A Few More Rounds

A Collection of Boxing Tales

Jerry Fitch and John J. Raspanti

I0154115

WIN BY
KO

Win By KO Publications
Iowa City

A Few More Rounds
A Collection of Boxing Tales

Jerry Fitch and John J. Raspanti

(ISBN-13): 978-1-949783-04-9

(softcover: 50# acid-free alkaline paper)

© 2020 by Jerry Fitch and John J. Raspanti

All Rights Reserved.

No part of this book may be reproduced, or transmitted in any form or by any means, graphic, electronic or mechanical, including photocopying, recording, taping, or by any information storage retrieval system without the written permission of Jerry Fitch, John J. Raspanti, and Win By KO Publications LLC.

Cover design by Gwyn Snider ©

Manufactured in the United States of America.

Win By KO Publications
Iowa City, Iowa
winbykopublications.com

Contents

FOREWORD

Jerry Fitch and John J. Raspanti met online, reviewing each other's books and formed a friendship that has resulted in *A Few More Rounds: A Collection of Boxing Tales*, a collaboration in which each contributed 10 chapters. Their love of the sport shines through on every page.

The strength of the book is the personal touch, stories not only about fights and fighters but about the authors' experiences that helped shape them as men, boxing fans and writers.

Fitch writes of a trip to Washington, D.C. in 1974 when he met former two-time middleweight champion Tony Zale at the front desk of the Mayflower Hotel. Zale was with his wife, Philomena, who the ex-champ referred to as "Mighty Mouth." Turned out that Tony was not the only athlete in the family. Philomena was a member of the All-American Women's Professional Baseball League, the subject of the 1992 movie, *A League of Their Own*.

When he was a boy Raspanti had a nasty encounter with a couple of racist at a barbeque. Two jerks asked him if he admired Cassius Clay (they refused to call him Muhammad Ali), and he nodded yes. Among the horrible things they said was that Clay should be lynched, or shot, or both. John's father, who had been a street fighter, boxed in the Chicago Golden Gloves and a big Joe Louis fan, intervened.

"He knew first-hand what it was like to admire a black man," wrote Raspanti. "As I gazed up at him, I also saw the street fighter he once was. It startled me. The stories about his brawling were hard for me to reconcile. He was Dad, who went to work dressed in a suit every day. It was hard for me to see him as a fighter. Now I could."

You don't hear much about former light heavyweight champion Anton Christoforidis, a native of Greece who for a few years fought out of Fitch's hometown of Cleveland. Jerry arranged an interview with Christoforidis and, although he wasn't Greek, Fitch became a favorite of the Greek community, which led to a many unexpected perks.

There are many more unique stories like these in *A Few More Rounds: A Collection of Boxing Tales*, a book by two writers who are keeping the flame of boxing burning bright.

Nigel Collins, Collegeville, Pennsylvania, July 2020

Acknowledgments

I must give a big shout out to my co-author, John Raspanti. This is my first time ever working with another author and John made it so easy. While we each have different stories and writing styles the one thing we do share is a passion for boxing. Thank you John.

As always my son Tad Fitch continues to be a big influence on me. He is a great writer who has been an author of many books on the Titanic and maritime history and always encourages me to keep writing.

Last but certainly not least I give kudos to my love Lynda, whose proof-reading always makes me look better.

Jerry Fitch

Working on this book with Jerry has been a rewarding experience. We both went into this project not sure what to expect, but I've thoroughly enjoyed every minute of it. Thank you, Jerry.

To my late parents, who told me to chase my dreams. I have and will. Miss you and love you. A shout out to my son Nick, who makes me proud. Thank you for believing in your old man.

Lastly, but not least, a big thank you to the most important ladies in my life, my love Dove, and my editor, Sharon McCormick. I would not be doing this without your help and support.

John J. Raspanti

Introduction

We have loved boxing our entire lives. For several years now the two of us have spent time reviewing each other's books. It has been fun and has offered each of us a chance to read books on boxing that were about different subjects and composed in a different writing style other than our own. This experience has been rewarding.

Because of this we discussed the idea of combining brand new stories together in a book that would offer a little something for everyone. We're from different eras, so our experiences have been unique and interesting.

We have tried to tell the history of various boxers and their fights while also including human interest and personal stories surrounding these fighters and events.

This is our first effort being co-authors. We hope you enjoy the stories as much as we did writing them.

Jerry Fitch

John J. Raspanti

June 23, 2020

Tony Zale

By Jerry Fitch

For a brief time in the mid-70s I had a relationship with Ed Sweeny, a plumbing and heating contractor from Cleveland. Ed had also gotten involved in staging both amateur and professional boxing matches locally. He had invented an electronic scoring system called Soctron and used this system during his fight cards. Ed had been a ring announcer for boxing events at the old Cleveland Arena for a number of years and it was obvious he really enjoyed the boxing scene.

Soctron involved enclosed booths that were located on three sides of the ring where the judges sat inside and scored the fight. On the back side of the ring facing the crowd a scoreboard was located that showed a running tally of the action in live time. The judges had controllers in each hand that allowed them to push a button when either fighter landed a punch. If I recall it took three hits to add up to a point on the scoreboard.

The judges were isolated and had on headsets that blocked out any crowd reaction or noise. During the fight all of the fans, fighters and cornermen knew exactly who was winning. It seemed like a good idea at the time but as with most everything involving men and electronics, the system didn't take into consideration the human error factor. It had flaws. I personally witnessed a fight card where the tally for one fighter added up like a pinball machine, giving the impression that at least one of the judges was going spastic with his button pushing or the button was stuck. More points were added up than punches could have possibly landed in my opinion. I also recall that the fighters corner on the short end of this scoring spree were going nuts as the tally literally took away the fight from their man.

However in October of 1974 I was asked by Ed Sweeny if I would like to take a trip to Washington, D.C. and show a film of his Soctron scoring system at an event being held at the famous Mayflower Hotel. A new organization was trying to launch a boxing league. The idea was to have teams from various cities compete against each other.

Trying to add credibility to the potential boxing league the organizers lined up three former champions; Jersey Joe Walcott, Ike Williams and Tony Zale. I don't believe these former fighters were being asked to fork up any money to be involved with the league.

My understanding was that the league would be using their name and fame and that the former champions would be paid a fee for the use of their monikers.

I did show the film Ed Sweeny put together of his Soctron invention. The film had two Cleveland amateur fighters putting on a sparring session. The footage showed how the scoring worked and explained all of the advantages of the system according to Ed Sweeny. I also gave a talk to the crowd about the Soctron system.

However months after this event my understanding was that Ed Sweeny apparently never heard any positive feedback from the group and then I realized the boxing league never got off the ground. I was actually hired after the event by Ed Sweeny and briefly worked as a ring announcer for his local Cleveland area fight shows. Even then the Soctron scoring system never caught on. After several more fight cards, the shows and Soctron went into obscurity.

One very special thing came out of the Washington, D.C. event for me personally. First I was able to renew my friendship with Jersey Joe Walcott, whom I had met for the first time ten years earlier. I had also never met Ike Williams, the former great lightweight champion so that was special. And last but certainly not least I met the former two-time middleweight champion Tony Zale for the first time. This encounter turned into one of those friendships that I could never have envisioned and it lasted for several years. I can say that even after all of these years it remains one of my fondest memories.

Most followers of boxing history know of Tony Zale. Perhaps best known for his trilogy of fights with Rocky Graziano, Tony was far more than the sum of those battles. His career as a fighter was impressive and his life before and after his ring days was very iconic.

Tony Zale was born Anthony Florian Zaleski on May 29, 1913 in Gary, Indiana, the sixth of seven children of Josef and Kataryna, Polish Immigrants. The whole story of his parents, the trials and tribulations of coming to a new country, the hardships, the hard work, is summed up beautifully in Thad (Ted) Zale and Clay Moyle's wonderful 2014 book *Tony Zale: The Man of Steel*. The book is 490 pages and is filled with countless photos and history about Tony Zale and his family. In my humble opinion it's the one and only book Zale fans will ever need to own.

His career was special and I am not about to rehash his great battles with so many tough opponents from Al Hostak, Billy Soose, Fred Apostoli, Steve Mamakos, Billy Conn and concluding with his last fight in 1948 against Marcel Cerdan. His final record was 67 wins (45 knockouts), 18 losses and 2 draws. A two-time World Middleweight Champion, Tony was someone whose career from the Golden Gloves to the pros left behind many opponents who wished they had not entered the ring with this tough man.

Tony had a history of working in the steel mills in Gary, Indiana and his service to our country in World War II in the Navy and later in the Army Reserves showed what a patriot he was. His honors both in the ring and out take up many pages in the Zale book. Tony hobnobbed with athletes and political leaders all the way to the Presidency. Everyone knew Tony Zale.

When I arrived at the Mayflower Hotel on that October day in 1974, I walked up to the front desk to check in and there stood Tony Zale and his wife, Philomena. As I mentioned I had never met Tony before but there was no mistaking who he was. Those chiseled cheekbones, those piercing eyes, the look was all too familiar. I knew who Tony Zale was, what boxing fan didn't?

Well, needless to say as they also checked into their room, I introduced myself and we agreed that we would talk later on. But one never knows exactly how such promises will play out. Luck would have it that I indeed would find the time to get Tony and Philomena alone before and after the dinner and activities. It turned out to be a very rewarding time and we eventually exchanged phone numbers and other information.

I didn't know it at the time but Zale family members, even Tony himself, referred to his wife Philomena as "Mighty Mouth." She was a hoot, didn't pull any punches and was obviously very protective of Tony. I eventually found out she was quite an athlete herself having played for the All-American Women's Professional Baseball League. She played for the Grand Rapid Chicks from 1945-1947. She was then traded to the Racine Belles in 1948. Philomena is in the record books as being the first woman to ever hit a home run out of Comiskey Park (Chicago), center field. In 1988, she, with the other living players, became immortalized in the "Women in Baseball" permanent display at the Baseball Hall of Fame in Cooperstown. The 1992 movie *A League of Their Own* was inspired by the true life women's league.

When I met Philomena, who was born Philomena Gianfrancisco, I realized she was someone who probably could rub some people the wrong way. She indeed had her opinions and was outspoken and often very loud but she always treated me with respect and I never had any issues with her.

On the second day in Washington D.C. there was a reception in one of the party rooms and we all had time to mingle. Jersey Joe Walcott and I rehashed old memories about Jimmy Bivins.

Ike Williams and I had a few moments. But the best memory I have from that time is initial conversations I had with Tony Zale. I found him very friendly and forthcoming. He really surprised me how he hammed it up with me when it came time to pose for a couple pictures. I will admit he startled me when he pretended to hit me with a right. I can't even imagine how hard he punched during his prime. Believe it or not in 1974 this man still looked hard as rock. Philomena was quick to point out that Tony worked out on a regular basis and still had the body of a young man. You could see how proud she was of him.

Although Tony and Philomena kept in touch after 1974, even exchanging Christmas greetings, we never were able to meet up in person. We did trade letters and an occasional phone call. I really didn't take any of this for granted.

I learned over time that Philomena was Tony's second wife. I got the feeling that perhaps some of Tony's family members didn't always appreciate how domineering she appeared when it came to Tony. In the Zale book however it tells that as the years went along the entire Zale family realized Philomena was good for Tony, she loved him and took care of him.

As the years passed I became more and more involved in boxing. I began to be part of an organization in Rochester, New York. It was called The Rochester Boxing Association. This group eventually morphed into The Rochester Boxing Hall of Fame but in the early days when I was personally involved it was called The Rochester Boxing Association.

After going to their first dinner in 1978, I was asked to help out the following year. Board members and the then president knew that I had met up with a lot of former boxing greats. Some of these fighters I met when I was writing my first articles for *Boxing Illustrated* and later *The Ring*. The group in addition to honoring upstate New York boxers with their own Hall of Fame, wanted to invite and honor former greats at their annual dinners with the Integrity Award and Courage Awards. They asked me to line up some legends if I could.

In 1979 I had my first shot at inviting former greats to the RBA as it was called. Cleveland's Jimmy Bivins was my friend and I felt he deserved any honor that could come his way. He seemed to be a forgotten great. I asked Jimmy and his wife Elizabeth if they would like to go to Rochester and be honored and they quickly agreed. I also was fortunate to get other family members, former Cleveland boxers and friends to attend the dinner.

My second thought for an honoree was Tony Zale. Tony was not a forgotten great but he too deserved all of the praise and honors that could possibly come his way. I called the Zale apartment in Chicago and after filling in Philomena about the particulars of the event (meaning flight and room were to be covered by the group), she handed the phone to Tony. He seemed very happy to be a part of the event in April of 1979.

Funny side story about that year. The previous year the Rochester Boxing Association had held their dinner in February. Anyone familiar with that part of the country knows that upstate New York gets a lot of bad weather in the winter. Buffalo and Rochester and many other places often get buried in snow. The group decided that to make it a safer bet to beat the weather they would move the dinner to April. Seemed like a smart move to me.

Best laid plans sometimes don't work out. A late winter storm hit. My normal four-and-a-half hour drive to Rochester from Cleveland took closer to seven hours. The Zale's plane from Chicago could not land in Rochester and had to be routed to New York City. They eventually made it to Rochester in time to make the dinner just as the rest of us did, but it was a bit hectic for a while.

For several years after that I lined up the honored fighters for the Rochester dinner. Among the fighters I landed besides Tony Zale and Jimmy Bivins were Jersey Joe Walcott, Jimmy McLarnin, Billy Conn, Earnie Shavers, Floyd Patterson and Pete Rademacher. With two major honorees during those years it was always a tough choice as to who I was to introduce at the dinner. I could only do one so I had to make the difficult decision and let the president or emcee introduce the second one. When it came to the 1979 dinner I had to go with my hometown friend, Jimmy Bivins. I wanted to honor Tony Zale too but I was sure he would get his just due no matter who was given the honor of introducing him. And Tony got a wonderful introduction.

I have to admit that although I was well aware of Tony's career I knew very little about his personal life when I first met him in 1974. I had a rare opportunity to talk one-on-one with Tony in 1979 while in Rochester. Although he had only met me less than five years before, he apparently felt comfortable enough to open up to me. In the basement of a friend that I was staying with in Rochester, the two of us looked at some of the memorabilia on the walls and also talked about his career. Then when the subject of his two marriages came up, Tony reflected on his often troubled first marriage, his years of not being able to see his children from that marriage and some rather troubling incidents that occurred while still married. Tony married his first wife Adeline on April 11, 1942, two days after he enlisted in the United States Navy. They divorced on December 15, 1951. All of this is covered in the Zale book so I feel no need to rehash it. However, I was amazed at how open Tony was and at the time I had never read anything about some of the things he told me that day. He did tell me some heart warming things about meeting Philomena where one day he, in a childlike way, touched her and said "Tag you're it." He said he knew she was the one for him. Tony and Philomena married on September 19, 1970, in Las Vegas.

After the dinner the Zales and I kept in touch on a fairly regular basis. Philomena always kept me informed about events they were going to, honors coming Tony's way, and I would send them any postings or stories I wrote on Tony in various publications. Philomena kept me informed of his various work with the Park System in Chicago, CYO and other events Tony and Philomena were involved in. I also learned how proud Tony was to be of Polish descent.

It made me feel good that my relationship with Tony Zale and his wife wasn't just a one-time thing that ended with a boxing dinner. It was special being able to call the Zales friends.

As a matter of fact we did meet up again in Los Angeles at the Cauliflower Alley Club and the World Boxing Hall of Fame dinner. It was fantastic seeing them again and perhaps if I didn't have such a crazy work schedule I may have been able to see them more often.

A very interesting thing happened in the summer of 1981. I read a one paragraph item buried in the back of a newspaper. It said that a man identified as Tony Zale, a great fighter, had been found dead in a trailer in Arizona. I couldn't believe that there wasn't more to the story if it were indeed true. So I thought about this and figured the only way to know for sure was to phone the Zale apartment in Chicago.

I called Tony's apartment and as the phone rang, I thought about what I would say, how I could be tactful yet still find out if the rumor was true. Philomena answered my call and after identifying myself, I asked her if I could speak to Tony. "Tony's sleeping," Philomena replied. "By the way, did you hear the rumor that Tony died?" It turned out that the man who died was an alcoholic drifter who had been impersonating Zale throughout the Sun Belt for 25 years, caging drinks.

I hooked up Bob Dolgan, award winning sports writer for the Plain Dealer, with the Zale family and he wrote a nice story on the whole incident mentioned above. This man in Arizona had been doing the Zale impersonation for many years and Philomena had received a call from a Texas newspaper six years before this episode. The paper had been suckered in and were about to be involved in a fund-raiser to pay for the hospital bills of an alcoholic who claimed to be Tony Zale. Tony Zale was a strict teetotaler and it was upsetting that anyone would think the alcoholic was him. The newspaper was calling to check and see if the man was the real Tony Zale "If my husband is down there, who's sleeping with me here?" Philomena wise-cracked.

As the years went by I would occasionally hear from Philomena and of course in time I was also made aware that Tony was slipping healthwise as life took its toll. Things really started to get worse in 1989 as Tony started to be confused on occasions. One time he even thought Philomena was his first wife, Adeine, according to Philomena.

Philomena was determined to keep Tony involved and rewarded for all of his good work both in and out of the ring. She sent me a photo postcard showing Tony being honored by President George H. W. Bush on October 16, 1990, with the President's Citizen Medal. Tony was in a wheelchair by then. All of us face the uncertainty of our health as we get older, not just old fighters. When Philomena died of cancer on January 18, 1992 I am sure a huge part of Tony died with her. Five years later on March 20, 1997, Tony joined Philomena.

After years of work Thad (Ted) Zale and Clay Moyle and Ted's wife Deb got their book into print and for sale in 2014. It is a beauty and I recommend it to any boxing fans, especially those who are fans of Tony Zale.

One last note: On November 5, 2015, a person or persons unknown at this writing broke into Canastota's International Boxing Hall of Fame and stole Tony Zale's two championship belts, along with four belonging to Carmen Basilio. And even though there are vast amounts of memorabilia in the museum, these were the only things taken. Award money was offered, Ted and Deb and daughter Haley have gone to great lengths to find the belts and get some satisfaction. As of now there has been no news regarding the whereabouts of the belts.

Dad, Oklahoma, And Cassius Clay/Muhammad Ali

By John J. Raspanti

I grew-up in a household where we often talked boxing since my dad and grandfather both loved the sport.

Dad competed in the Chicago Golden Gloves in the 1940s. He often said that his nose, which leaned to the left, was a by-product of his days in the ring. When Grampa was a teenager, he'd prowl around the outskirts of Chicago looking for places to mix it up. He'd eventually find "bouts" and join in. Think of local tough man contests. He wanted the extra change, and liked fighting. Heavyweight champion Jack Dempsey inspired him. He fought like the "Manassa Mauler," wading in and letting his hands go.

Dad was more a boxer-puncher. His fighting career began on the south side of Chicago. He was taller than most, and a good athlete. His fighting in the streets was more for territory and survival. He was seven when he first heard the name Joe Louis. The legendary "Brown Bomber" had made his debut in the Windy City in 1934. Dad learned that Louis would be fighting King Levinsky a year later at Comiskey Park, located eight blocks from the tiny street-level apartment Dad lived in with his parents and six siblings.

He was desperate to go, but didn't have money for a ticket. Most people didn't since the Great Depression had knocked the country on its heels. And many in his Italian neighborhood didn't like his devotion to Louis. Grampa was now a husband and father, working at a grocery store in the produce department. He didn't fight as much anymore. Grandma didn't like it. Grampa still did, but devoted his time to Chicago fighters he admired, like lightweight champion Barney Ross.

In 1937, Dad read that Louis would be fighting "The Cinderella Man," heavyweight champion James J. Braddock, again at Comiskey Park. No way he was going to miss it this time, ticket or not. Armed with only a penny in his pocket, he was off, determined to find a way into the park. As he got closer to Comiskey, he could see the lights and hear a rumbling. Excitement was in the air. He knew the park well, having sold newspapers there for close to a year. He spotted two ticket sellers by the entrance. Suddenly he heard a roar from inside the park. Had the Louis-Braddock fight started? He picked up his step, nearing the open entrance. Maybe the ticket guys wouldn't see him. One did.

"Hey, where do you think you're going?" Dad was caught. He was so close. He could hear the crowd muttering. He thought of running. The voice belonged to an older, heavy-set man who wasn't smiling. His cohort wasn't smiling either.

"I just want to see the Louis fight," Dad said. Another roar shook the arena. The man's eyes softened. "You go ahead, son," he said. Dad, crouching in an aisle, made it just in time to see Louis knock out Braddock to win the title.

Fast forward twenty-seven years later. I'm mesmerized by this guy named Cassius Clay. His fast hands, and even faster mouth, have me fascinated. Is there anything he can't do? To me, he's a real Superman. Two years later we're living in Tulsa, Oklahoma. I'm a full-fledged boxing fan. Every month, I bugged Mom to take me to a local liquor store to purchase *The Ring* magazine. She did.

By then, Cassius Clay had officially changed his name to Muhammad Ali. His nickname, "The Louisville Lip," fit like a proverbial glove. He had won the heavyweight championship from Sonny Liston in an improbable upset. He fought Liston again, stopping him in the first round with something called an anchor punch.

He bragged and made predictions, but I always saw a twinkle in his eye. Most in the south didn't. I had no idea how controversial he was. He was amusing. In my little town, I was slowly becoming aware of the hatred Ali inspired. I knew of only one heavyweight from Oklahoma. His name was Carl Morris. They called him "The Oklahoma White Hope." He was big and slow but could punch. He beat a number of ranking heavyweights of his time, but not former sparring partner, and future heavyweight champion of the world, Jack Dempsey. "The Manassa Mauler" defeated Morris three times in 1917 and 1918.

By the end of the summer of 1967, my learning curve had improved dramatically, due to an incident that occurred during a neighborhood barbecue. I can remember hearing my name and running over to where four or five neighborhood dads stood. They were eating catfish and drinking beer. Lots of laughter. The mothers were talking on the other side of the street. I could see my mom, but had no idea where my dad was. I stood and waited.

One of the fathers put his plate down and asked me if I knew who Cassius Clay was. (They refused to use his Muslim name) I nodded. I saw them glance at each other. I could feel some tension. Did I admire Clay, he asked? I nodded again. They mumbled. They told me what a terrible person "Clay" was. How he was a communist. I shook my head. They said he should be lynched, or shot, or both. They used an ugly word that starts with an n. I felt two hands rest on my shoulders, as I heard my father say:

"My son can like whoever he likes. I'd appreciate it if you kept that kind of language to yourselves." Their heads bobbed ever so slightly. They never bothered me again. Dad had come to my rescue, sympathizing with my plight.

He knew first-hand what it was like to admire a black man. As I gazed up at him, I also saw the street fighter he once was. It startled me. The stories about his brawling were hard for me to reconcile. He was Dad, who went to work dressed in a suit every day. It was hard for me to see him as a fighter. Now I could.

The Greeks

By Jerry Fitch

Cleveland has had its share of excellent fighters over the years. Some were homegrown like Johnny Kilbane, others moved to the Cleveland area with their family at a very early age. Among those were standouts like Jimmy Bivins, Lloyd Marshall, Johnny Risko and Georgie Pace.

And sometimes fighters even came from Europe as was the case of Anton Christoforidis, a Greek born fighter. He eventually made the Cleveland area his home during many prime fights of his career.

Anton Christoforidis was born on May 26, 1917, in Messinia, Greece. His professional boxing career started in 1934 in Athens. By the time he came to the United States, prior to the outbreak of World War II, he had participated in 46 fights and won 32 while losing 8 and drawing in 6. The majority of his fights were held in Paris. He also won and lost the European Middleweight Title, winning it against Bep Van Klaveren and losing it to Edouard Tenet.

As the war was closing in, Anton moved to the US and had five fights in New York, Detroit and Chicago, winning them all. He then got an offer to fight in Cleveland against former AAU and Golden Gloves Champion Jimmy Reeves on October 22, 1940. He knocked out Reeves in the second round. Finishing out 1940 Anton met up with Cleveland sensation, Jimmy Bivins, first losing a decision on November 18th, then handing Bivins his first career loss on December 2nd, both over ten rounds.

The Bivins win launched Anton into a title fight for the vacant NBA Light-heavyweight Title against Melio Bettina on January 13, 1941. Anton emerged the victor over fifteen rounds. It was a big win for Anton and Cleveland fans, especially the local Greek community. They looked at Anton as one of their own with a sense of pride.

Anton had a couple non-title fights in Baltimore and St. Louis before defending his NBA title against Gus Lesnevich in New York on May 22, 1941, in New York. He lost his title via a 15-round decision to the always tough Lesnevich.

After he lost his portion of the title, Anton had eleven more fights with mixed results. He had a quality win against Ceferino Garcia on one of the famous Cleveland News Toyshop Fund

Shows on December 1, 1941. In 1942 he got stopped in three rounds by the great Ezzard Charles. He then defeated Mose Brown and drew with Nate Bolden. In February 1943 he lost to Jimmy Bivins over fifteen rounds for the "Duration" Light-heavyweight title.

His next fight on April 21, 1943 saw Anton get soundly defeated by another Cleveland standout, Lloyd Marshall. Anton told me in 1981 that he felt he only really lost one fight in Cleveland and that was the Marshall fight. Although he respected Jimmy Bivins as a fighter he felt both of his losses to Jimmy were hometown decisions. In his career in Cleveland Anton had eleven fights and won eight. His only losses were to Bivins and to Marshall.

Anton had come to America to become a citizen and as World War II arrived he joined the US Navy and served during 1944-45. When he was discharged in 1946 he went back to boxing but didn't have the same fire. He won two and lost two through 1947, being stopped twice, once by Steve Belloise and in his final bout against Anton Raadik. His final record was 52-15-7.

After his boxing career came to a halt Anton and his wife remained in the Cleveland area and he opened a bar/restaurant in Geneva, Ohio, east of Cleveland. He loved to mingle with people and he also loved to hunt.

Anton and his wife got divorced in 1961. He sold his interests in Geneva in 1968 and moved to Florida to retire. In 1971 he took an extended trip back to Greece for the first time since he left there. It was supposed to be 45 days but it turned into 15 years!

I never was able to meet Anton while he lived in the Cleveland area. But in 1981 I noticed an article in the Plain Dealer saying he had come to Cleveland to visit old friends. He was staying at Swingos in downtown Cleveland which was a hotel and restaurant run by Nick and Jim Swingos, father and son Greeks and former friends of Anton when he lived in the Cleveland area.

Swingos was a famous venue because when bigtime entertainers came to town they usually stayed there. The list is long but Elvis Presley and Frank Sinatra were two of the biggest names along with rock bands such as Led Zeppelin. It was also a gathering place for local Greeks, a tight-knit community.

I called Swingos and asked to be put through to Anton's room. The phone rang and rang and there was no answer so I left a message. I didn't hear from him that day so I waited and hoped he would return my call. Later that night he did and asked me if I would meet him in the lobby of the hotel the next day.

When I arrived the next day I didn't see Anton in the lobby at the appointed time but in a short while he appeared from the dining room area. After introductions he invited me back to the dining room. Seated at a big table were Nick and Jim Swingos and a few other men, none of which I knew. After introducing me I quickly realized I was the only non-Greek there.

We had a nice conversation and every so often someone would say something to Anton in Greek and sometimes he laughed other times he didn't. However they did translate some of what was said to me. Unfortunately I am refraining from saying much in this story because it didn't really pertain to boxing and was very colorful.

One of the gentlemen at the table was a man named Ted Gregory. Ted was a Greek restaurant owner from the Cincinnati, Ohio area. He too had traveled up to Cleveland when he heard Anton Christoforidis was in town. He was a very friendly guy who owned a famous rib joint in Montgomery, Ohio called The Montgomery Inn. Not only was it famous for its barbecue but also for the clientele that frequented the place. On the wall were autographed photos and memorabilia of former Ohio State football greats such as Archie Griffin and baseball greats such as Pete Rose and Johnny Bench.

After an entertaining time we all left for the day but I was told that the next day Anton and Ted and a few others would be hanging out at the Statler Hotel, also in downtown Cleveland. The Swingos family had a second restaurant there.

When I showed up in the afternoon I saw Anton and Ted Gregory sitting at the bar so I walked over and they asked me to join them. During our conversation Ted Gregory told me he had a horse that was running her maiden race at the local harness track outside of Cleveland. I noticed several of the restaurant staff, who were also Greek, were talking about the horse. Ted said the odds were pretty high but he was told the horse had a very good chance of winning. It appeared to me that Ted was going to place some bets for the staff members. He asked me if I wanted to put a few bucks on the race but, because I hardly knew Ted, I decided to decline. Big mistake on my part. The horse whose name was Cinci-Maddie (in honor of his city and wife) came in 1st and paid a pretty good price.

Wait...it gets better as I like to say. I had plans to take my family down to Kings Island in Cincinnati, the following week. Kings Island was a fairly new amusement park in the Montgomery area where Ted lived. I happened to mention this to Ted and he promptly asked me what I thought at the time was a very strange question. He said, "Do you pay when you go there?" Those who know me probably would think I'd respond with some sort of quirky answer like "No I climb over the fence after the park closes." Of course I didn't say that.

I know I say it all the time and some readers of my books probably think I overuse one particular statement. But I can't help it, I have been blessed to be in the right place at the right time quite often. This was another time I can say that! I finally answered that of course I had to pay when I went to Kings Island. He said, "Not this time you aren't"! Ted informed me that when we got to the park we should go up to the Customer Service booth and give my name. So I did and the young lady smiled and handed me passes for the entire family. We had a great time. The young lady also asked me if we were coming to the Montgomery Inn that night to eat and I said probably. She said she worked there also as a hostess.

After a wonderful day at the park we went back to the hotel, cleaned up and headed to the restaurant. When we got there I thought we might have made a mistake as the line to get it went around the corner. But as I looked in I saw the girl who had worked at Kings Island and she waved us in. As we passed through I am sure the people in line wondered how we rated. We were escorted to the bar area for drinks. Before long we were taken to a nice table in one of the back rooms. We ordered our food and it was excellent. Later we were waiting for our waitress to bring us our bill. She had vanished into another room so we waited. Finally I caught her attention and she walked over. I told her we were finished and ready to leave. She smiled and said that the bill was taken care of by Ted's son. We were totally surprised and extremely grateful. As we left and passed the young hostess, she said "see you tomorrow at the park." She informed me we had passes for the second day also.

This story does not end there. In the fall of the same year, 1981, my family and I attended the Cleveland Rib Cook-off which was held every fall. Ted Gregory had never entered his Montgomery ribs at this event but got talked into it by his local Cleveland friends. We spotted him and he waved us over. His booth was adorned with photos of famous people who had loved Ted's ribs including Bob Hope and the Greek Ambassador to the United States. Well, we ordered some ribs from Ted and he would not accept a dime.

As the next couple of years went by I tried to find a way to show my appreciation to Ted Gregory. Jimmy Bivins had located one of his fights with Anton Christoforidis on 16mm film. The great Jim

Jacobs did not have this particular fight in his massive collection. I found out that Jim Jacobs did however have two of Anton's fights from Europe. I was able to allow Jim Jacobs to copy my film and as compensation he made two copies of the European fights and the Bivins' fight on one reel. So I did get to compensate Ted Gregory with a copy and also was eventually able to give a copy to Anton Christoforidis.

Anton went back to Greece and we kept in touch. I still have some of his letters which I have kept all these years. He loved to remind me during our cold months in Cleveland how he was in short sleeves golfing in Greece. Among his golfing friends were many of the rich and famous residents of Greece.

Anton died in November of 1986 in Athens.

Dreams Come Alive At The Ring Of Fire

By John J. Raspanti

A few years ago, a friend told me about this place, "You have to see." His eyes lit up describing it. Curious, I made the trek across San Francisco Bay to find out why. I quickly figured out what he meant.

What I found was a small gem that lies within the sprawling landscape of of a San Francisco park. The Ring of Fire Boxing Club houses a roughly half the size of a regular squared circle. Outside the ropes are four heavy bags. The walls are painted dark, but the place is clean. The gym was born a number of years ago through the hard work and dedication of former local amateur boxing sensation, Jimmy Ford, who wanted to give all types of kids-rich and poor-a place to go.

"I used to box, and I had a gym when I was a little kid," said Ford in 2011. "Someone gave to me and mentored me when I was young. So it was time to give some of that back."

Ford was something of a Mozart with boxing gloves, attaining the highest ranking of any boxer at age 12. He boxed through his teen years, eventually capturing the San Francisco Golden Gloves. After recovering from personal battles outside the ring, Jimmy laced up the gloves again to raise money for a new boxing establishment.

"I had a beautiful career," he said with a wry smile. "I made it to the nationals and won the Golden Gloves in nineteen ninety-two. It's been a real journey. I've been in this game since I was ten years old."

In his forties now, Ford never gave up on the idea of starting a gym near his old stomping grounds. He started working with some kids with the help of his old trainer. Roaming around the giant complex known as Crocker Amazon Park, he stumbled across a storage facility and asked if he could train his students there.

"I came in here and it was a disaster," he said. "I was working for the parks and recreation at that time, so I unloaded everything, bought some boxing equipment from World Gym, and got the ball rolling."

Ford worked six days a week training his students. Near exhaustion, he asked trainer and former boxer, Miguel Rios, to help him with the kids. Rios readily agreed.

Soon thereafter John Fuentes joined the team as the gym manager. The San Francisco Fire Department also became involved, donating money and merchandise. For Fuentes, just finding the small half of a gym was a challenge. He remembers wandering around until in the distance he heard a bell.

Fuentes had his own gym in the City and trained such local fighters as Shantile Jordan and welterweight contender Karim Mayfield. But to him, the powerful potential of the place that would be called the "Ring of Fire" was the day he took on a troubled kid

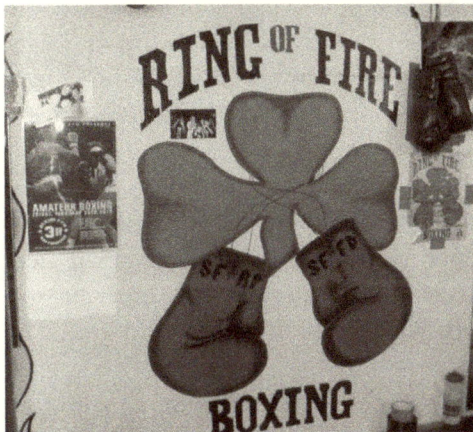

who had been in twenty-one different foster homes. "I took him under my wing and he started boxing," Fuentes said. "He turned out to be a six-day-a-week kid, so I had to be here. I saw something in him."

What Fuentes saw was the real deal, as the kid with the problems went on to win the Oxnard novice division title and, a few months later, made it all the way to the Golden Gloves finals. The kid could fight. "I tell all the kids that if you quit here, you quit somewhere else." Fuentes knows about the temptation out on the streets. "I tell them, you can't come here and be in trouble. If you love this, don't do that."

In the long history of boxing, many of the greatest fighters started their careers in places similar to the Ring of Fire. Before he was Muhammad Ali, the young Cassius Clay began to box in a basement gym in Louisville, Kentucky. The legendary Joe Louis discovered boxing at the Brewster Recreation Center in Detroit, Michigan. Small, cramped, and ugly to some, Brewster's became the home away from home for Louis, and another youngster whose birth name was Walker Smith, but who would be reborn as Sugar Ray Robinson. It's a sobering thought to consider that without that basement gym in Kentucky, and Brewster's, the boxing world might not have witnessed the amazing exploits of Ali, Louis, and Robinson. Without the place, the hope dies.

Ford, Rios, and Fuentes find the team aspect of Fire one of the most rewarding things they do. They're exciting times when the boxing team hits the road. Fuentes sums it up best. "Kids that have never left the city are getting on airplanes and flying to the Midwest. "Each boxer competes in a different weight class. They get a sense of team, they hang out together," said Fuentes.

The tournaments are in Oxnard, Kansas City, and a smaller venue in Reno. The results have been favorable for the participants of the little gym that could. The success of the Fire boxing team attracted kids from in and around the Bay Area. The team has produced National Amateur champions Charley Sheeny, Joe Gumina, and Nick Chamoun. As much as Ford, Diaz, and Fuentes welcomed more kids, the size of their gym was making it more and more difficult to maneuver. They began to search for a larger facility. They found a dilapidated autoshop in Brisbane and in a matter of months, with the help of many friends, converted the shop into a working gym.

A full-size ring sits in the center of the gym, with a locker room nearby and a balcony overhead. One day soon, the Ring of Fire kids will be fighting here in their own gym. But Fuentes makes it clear that the original gym, marked with grit, desire and character will never close. "The Crocker gym will always be open and free," he says smiling.

The beauty of this sentiment is two-fold. Three men, all with full-time jobs and boxing backgrounds, giving their time and their souls to young adults, troubled or not who can dream the impossible, and perhaps, just maybe, achieve it.

"I just wanted to give back to the community. The community gave it to me so now's my turn to give it back."
Jimmy Ford

"We never shut the door on anybody."
John Fuentes

A few years after I wrote this article, Jimmy Ford opened up the new The Ring of Fire Gym a few thousand feet from the old location. Both gyms flourish to this day.

More Jimmy Bivins

By Jerry Fitch

As the years have gone by and most of the honors have been given to Jimmy Bivins even after his death, I still try to keep young and old fans aware of how good he was. I am surprised in many ways how many don't know Jimmy. Yet I am often surprised when I see postings about him in a very positive light by many other fight fans and writers.

I guess I will always find little pieces of information or dig out facts I have never written about. For example, recently I realized that even though Jimmy had 112 professional fights there seems to be bits and pieces I still discover about him. He is the fighter I have written about the most in my years of writing about boxing. I wrote features on him in *The Ring* magazine, *Boxing News* (London), *Boxing Illustrated* and several other major magazines back in the day. I have written about Jimmy in chapters in several of my books, and have a separate volume on him titled "James Louis Bivins...The Man Who Would Be Champion." (2011 Tora Book Publishing) However since that book came out I am still finding stories I feel should be told when it comes to Jimmy Bivins. Not all of them are happy but they are part of his life and legacy.

During my years with Jimmy he was often interviewed by newspaper people or just historians in general. He used to crack me up when he would tell people, "Hey ask Jerry Fitch, he knows more about me than I do."

I never actually claimed to know more about this fine man than he knew about himself. I did however spend considerable time scanning through newspaper articles, microfilm, and eventually other sources when I finally got a computer in the 1990s. Needless to say I picked Jimmy's brain most times we were together.

In the 1970s Jimmy allowed me to take his scrapbooks and copy anything I wanted. I also did some minor repairs on some of the torn pages and photos. I gave them back to him but who knows what happened to them. More on that later.

As I traveled more and more I did meet up with some of Jimmy's former opponents. Some were obvious like Cleveland's Joey Maxim. But I did meet up with several others in person such as Joe Louis, Jersey Joe Walcott, Lloyd Marshall, Archie Moore, Johnny Flynn, Ezzard Charles, Clarence Henry, Anton

Christoforidis, and Charley Burley. A few others, like Coley Wallace, I either corresponded with or talked to on the telephone. I picked up a lot of insight from them, most of which I have written about in my articles and books.

Some stories I was not able to write about in my 2011 book. Recently I have seen some videos and picked up some interesting things on the computer in various boxing sites.

When Jimmy Bivins fought Ezzard Charles in 1948, in a heavyweight eliminator for the vacant heavyweight title after Joe Louis retired the first time, there were several things beyond the actual fight that are worth writing about. One of the stories Jimmy actually told me about the 1948 fight was that black fans were being discriminated against when it came to where they could sit at Griffith Stadium in Washington D.C. Although Jimmy and Ezzard were opponents they also were friends from their amateur days and had a common goal, to not allow this to happen. According to Jimmy they threatened to not go on with the fight if this practice continued. The fight went on so I assume at least some changes were made.

Something else I never had read or heard about, and neither Jimmy nor anyone else ever told me in all the years I knew him, was something that I viewed recently in Dick Cavett's three-part interview of the great trainer Ray Arcel. I found it on Youtube. In Part Two, Ray tells a 1948 story, when he was training Jimmy Bivins for his fight with Ezzard Charles. I never knew Ray Arcel had trained Jimmy for that fight. Arcel tells of how they wanted to put Jimmy and him in a fleabag hotel because Jimmy was black. The ever sharp Arcel would not go for that and he knew a friend who managed a nicer hotel nearby. When they went in Ray told the man at the desk that Jimmy was his valet. The guy looked at them in disbelief, saying he had heard everything. Ray said he told the man at the desk that when they ordered food he would hide Jimmy in the bathroom. But the man told him he could only order for one person. So he told Ray that what he could do was order the food, let Jimmy have that and he, Ray could eat in the coffee shop. Sad but true story. I guess with it being 1948 America, none of this should surprise me.

Jimmy always was honest with me, he didn't sugar coat things and he also was not the type of guy who would bad mouth something unless it was just necessary. I never felt he was exaggerating when he told me a story because he had no need to. Jimmy said he was approached more than once by "the powers that be" to "play ball" with them. In other words they wanted to sink their hooks into him, control him, who knows what else they would have demanded. He refused and many feel that certainly added to the fact he never was offered a title fight regardless of his ranking in either division. Jimmy also claimed that when his 1948 fight with Ezzard Charles ended and the ring announcer announced the winner, he practically whispered it. Although I have the complete fight and there is sound as far as fans yelling things, and the referee giving the fighters instructions, telling them to break and to mix it up, unfortunately the video does not have the ring announcers voice at the end, you only see the referee raising Charles's hand. However you can hear fans booing the decision in Charles favor.

I suppose those who knew Jimmy long before me might have a few stories I was not privy to when I started writing about Mr. Bivins. I know according to newspaper accounts there were more than a few people who felt Jimmy was sort of uppity, that he was arrogant in some ways. Honestly I am not doubting some of Jimmy's actions when he was very young were on the cocky side. He was good, confident in what he did and I suppose back then a bit of a show off. By the time I met Jimmy in the 60s he probably was a lot more reserved than during his early years. However I am also not naive, when I read some stories, especially by some of the newspaper men back then it was not hard to read between the lines. Being biased is one thing, being prejudice is another.

I am not one to cast stones at anyone, especially when I consider the fact my life has been far from perfect. Having tasted the sting of failed relationships I know it is not easy. But my failures didn't end up in the sports page.

Jimmy was married three times and his second marriage is the one that was fodder for the local news. While married to the former Dollree Mapp they had more than their share of controversy. Court filings were part of the public viewing with each side blaming the other, eventually each side filing for divorce and each sending out accusations, some rather nasty.

On top of all this when Jimmy Bivins and Archie Moore fought for the first time on August 22, 1945 in Cleveland Municipal Stadium, Dollree and Jimmy were still legally married. During this fight Dollree was sitting ringside cheering for ol' Archie. Apparently they had a thing going. This infuriated Jimmy and not only did he proceed to inflict a whipping on Archie, he also hit him after he knocked him down in the second round. He stood over him and clobbered him with an uppercut. According to Archie Moore,

behind the ear. The Cleveland Boxing Commission gave Moore a five minute rest and awarded him the round on a foul. But after three trips to the canvas in the second Moore went down twice in the 5th round and once more in the 6th where he was counted out.

Dollree Mapp Bivins and Jimmy did get divorced and it is believed she took a huge chunk of money from Jimmy. Dollree Mapp is probably remembered more for a court case that came about in 1961. Mapp was involved in the numbers racket in Cleveland. At the time Don King ran his own numbers game by paying local racketeer Shondor Birns $200 a week. In 1957 a bomb blast splintered Don King's front porch to kindling wood, according to a July 9, 1984 *Plain Dealer* article by James Neff. King told a local vice cop, Carl Delau that "Shondor Birns did this." King apparently owed Birns money but it was never proved that he was involved with the bombing of King's porch.

Delau wanted to put the squeeze on Birns and during his rounds his partner saw a car of a numbers guy parked at a house where Dollree Mapp lived. The article mentioned that Dollree had been married to Jimmy Bivins and later engaged to Archie Moore and that she also worked the edges of the numbers racket.

It was pretty common in those days for police to enter a house if they felt they had probable cause. Three Cleveland cops busted into Dollree Mapp's house, claimed they had a warrant, which they didn't and found gambling paraphernalia and some obscene literature. The police didn't actually have a warrant but she was arrested anyway on two different charges and eventually sentenced to 1-7 years in jail. While she was out on bond a young local lawyer took the issue to court, saying that her civil liberties were violated and her Fourth Amendment rights, "the right of the people to be secure in their persons houses, papers and effects against unreasonable searches…shall not be violated and no Warrants shall issue but upon probable cause supported by Oath" were violated. This had been on the books since 1914 but hardly ever followed. The case became a landmark case in 1961 - *Mapp vs. Ohio*. The police didn't like it, felt it hindered their jobs, allowed a lot of bad guys to get off, that their hands would be tied and that crime would rise. In 1984 the Supreme Court stripped a precedent that, in part, was established by the Mapp case. I have no idea how it stands today.

There is much more to the Mapp story, but this chapter is about her former husband Jimmy Bivins. I can say however that she and Archie Moore never got married and she eventually sued Archie for breach of promise. Dollree actually outlived Jimmy Bivins, dying in October of 2014 in Georgia. NOTE: Jimmy never had much to say about Dollree, other than to mutter, "Dollree was something else."

Since Jimmy Bivins died on July 4, 2012 several things happened. First of all his funeral ended up being a sad situation because basically there wasn't one. Visitation was set up by family members locally, namely his nephew and his wife, and other close family. But before any of us could show up at the funeral home, visitation was cancelled by his daughter, who lived out of town at the time. Those who knew the history of Jimmy Bivins and how he was abused by his own immediate family and was found living in filth in the attic of his daughter and son-in-laws house in April of 1998, probably weren't shocked. He weighed just 110 lbs. at the time the Cleveland Police found him and rescued him from near death. It was a front page story in the *Plain Dealer* and eventually was written about in Sports Illustrated and other publications.

Still it came as a surprise to most of us because we all thought that chapter of his life was over. Not only was the visitation cancelled but also the gravesite was moved. Nobody was allowed to attend, a court order was issued and deputies stood by the gravesite to make sure nobody attended who wasn't invited.

Later on I was fortunate to be one of the guest speakers at a memorial service at Liberty Hill Baptist Church, the Bivins family church for many years. As former award winning *Plain Dealer* writer Dan Coughlin wrote in a July 26th 2012 article, *"We finally said goodbye to former boxing great Jimmy Bivins this past Saturday. There were less than 100 people in Liberty Hill Baptist Church at E. 82nd and Euclid Ave. because of the confusion caused by Jimmy's nutty daughter, Josetta Banks, who cancelled his wake and earlier funeral. Many people missed the notice when it was rescheduled."*

How someone could do such harmful things to their own father is beyond any comprehension I have. Jimmy and his third wife Elizabeth took such good care of their daughter. As a matter of fact they had custody of three of her children for a number of years. Yet the daughter ruined it for so many fans and friends and other family members in the end. I mean how could she not allow people to pay their respects and say goodbye? We may never know.

There have been some nice surprises in the years since Jimmy passed. However even those have ended up being disappointing in some cases. A street near where Jimmy went to high school off of East 38th, on Cleveland's Eastside, was named Bivins Way by the City of Cleveland. Unfortunately they spelled his name wrong on the sign, spelling it Bivens. When I found out after stopping there to see it, I contacted the city officials in charge of such things and they assured me the street sign would be changed, that it was an easy task. Later they informed me that because the people living there had their lease agreements, utility bills and all other legal documents listed as Bivens, it would be too much trouble. So it has stayed as Bivens.

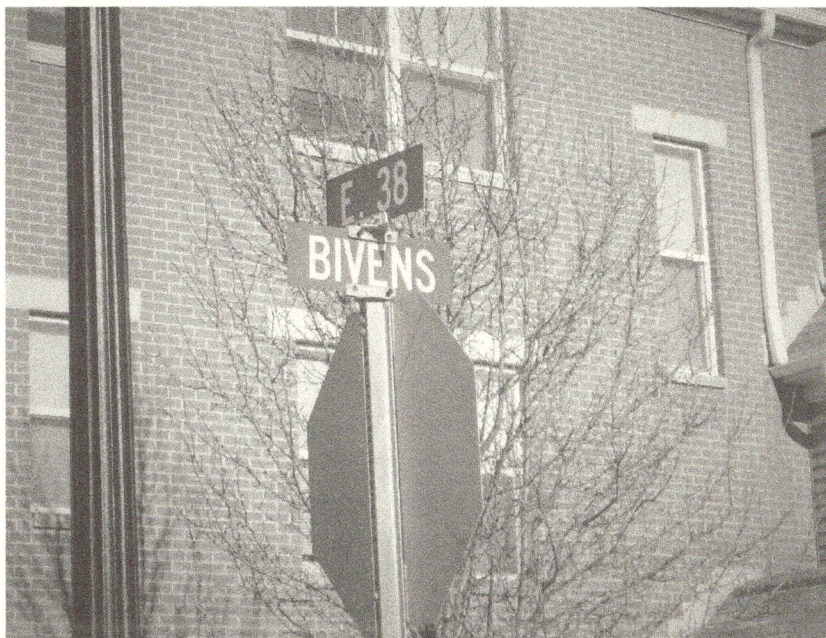

There was a park across the street from the Old Angle Gym, where Jimmy had himself once trained, where he trained fighters and later became part owner. The Old Angle Gym was a part of Cleveland boxing history, located in the same area where Johnny Kilbane had once grown up. When that gym was torn down in 1975, Jimmy moved his gym to West 30th and Bridge Avenue in the West Side Community Center. In 1978 he moved into a building that was part of St. Malachi Catholic Church right across from where the famous Old Angle Gym had stood. He remained there until 1996 when his health started to fade and his family situation started to apparently erode.

In 2000, the City of Cleveland decided to name that park across the street from where the Old Angle had been, in Jimmy's name. However it turned out the park had already been named in honor of another man, a local politician named Bernard "Brick" Materson, who died in 1918. Local Ward 14 Councilman Nelson Cintron went ahead with the legislation anyway. But no plaque or signage was ever displayed. Recently the area was redeveloped as an apartment complex.

My memories of Jimmy are good ones. The stories of how he helped many people, how he put his own money to work keeping his gyms open, how he was robbed by a young man on the bakery truck he drove after retirement and that he went to court and asked the judge for leniency and told the judge he would take the youngster under his wing at the gym.

I remember how generous Jimmy was to me, how he invited my family to events on his dime, how he came out to my house and cooked for friends and family with his famous ribs and fixings.

I remember how he and his wife Elizabeth came out to our house when my son Tad was born with a trunk load of baby gifts. That is the kind of guy he was and friend he was. Some people claimed he was "cheap" but I certainly never saw that in all the years I knew him.

I think back fondly on a few road trips we took to dinners and Hall of Fame events, how we talked on the phone. If he wasn't at his house or the gym he was over at his mother Fleda's house a street away. After his father died and for years after, I would call the house and his elderly mother Fleda would answer. Before she would hand the phone to Jimmy or tell me he wasn't there, she would always say, "Jerry can you find me a young man? A little over twenty-one, with money."

Another thing I recently discovered was that Jimmy Bivins, although he had 112 professional fights, in only six of those fights did his opponent have a losing record, and three of those came in his first year as a pro in 1940. Boxing was different then, fighters had to fight a lot and often never made it to the top of the heap.

Since the Bivins book came out I have also scanned through old newspaper and magazine articles. It never ceases to amaze me how more than a few writers were so critical of Jimmy and yet I keep finding many positive things like where he was ranked in top ten of the heavyweight standings in the later years of his career. Nobody can ever argue that Jimmy wasn't the same fighter he was prior to going into the Army. The Bivins of the early 1940s was simply amazing, even great. He did have some quality wins after coming out of the service in 1944, especially in 1945. But he was different. His sister Maria always said the beating he took from the Military Police in the Army did some permanent damage. That story was barely mentioned back then.

What surprises even me, however, is that although the majority of Jimmy's losses happened from February of 1946 until his retirement in late 1955, twenty of his twenty-five career losses in fact, he was still very relevant in the heavyweight picture during that time. Young fans now most likely wouldn't have a clue who these guys were that Jimmy was matched with at the end of his career. However he was mostly fighting contenders or up and coming fighters. And he did have some real quality wins.

Scanning articles I read that Jimmy was as high as #2 in the heavyweight division in 1948, still as high as #5 in 1949. Even in 1952 he was in the top ten. He was good enough to be highly ranked but apparently never good enough in the promoters eyes to warrant a shot at the title.

It pleases me to now see many websites on Facebook give praise to Jimmy and his career. More than a few historians and writers have posted articles stating Jimmy was one of the greatest fighters to never win a title. Others have ranked him very high in the all time light-heavyweight listings, a division he really shined in.

As for me... I was not around during Jimmy's career, way too young to actually have seen him fight. I only know what I have read, seen on film and video and from what I have heard from former opponents. I have extensively read not only the old newspaper clippings and magazine articles, I have also searched through microfilm at our local library.

I really don't care what others said about Jimmy. Whether he rubbed people the wrong way at times with his attitude may be true in some cases. I only know what I know from spending many years with him and seeing his acts of kindness and his contributions to the youth of the Cleveland area. He was one of our local sports heroes for sure and a good man.

I have made it my mission to keep Cleveland fighters and boxing history remembered and respected for all that it gave to boxing and us as fans and to our city in general. As far as James Louis Bivins... as long as I am alive I will personally keep his name alive. It is my honor to do so.

Hanging In The Fillmore District With A Welterweight Contender

By John J. Raspanti

On a rainy night in 2011, I went to a delicatessen in San Francisco, California, to meet a fighter and talk about his career.

I was introduced to Karim Mayfield the year before at a gym across the bay in Oakland. At that time, I was to interview future world champion Andre Ward, but ended up striking up a conversation with the likeable Mayfield. I had seen him dismantle Roberto Valenzuela a few months before at Oakland's Oracle Arena. He packed power in his right hand.

Now, Mayfield was preparing to fight Francisco Santana on the undercard of Ward's bout with Mikel Kessler. He had edged Santana by majority decision the year before. A rematch was set six months later. Santana wanted revenge. His only loss at that point had been to Mayfield.

I was struck by how confident Mayfield was. Like most fighters I've met, he was brutally honest and forthcoming. He knew what to expect from Santana. He smiled a lot, relishing the match.

A week later at Oracle, Mayfield fought Santana again. I was ringside to cover the fights for doghouseboxing. I arrived early to make sure I wouldn't miss any of the undercard bouts. The arena was nearly empty when the fights began. Mayfield and Santana threw hands 45 minutes before the main. With his family cheering him on, Mayfield stopped the favored Santana in round five.

I talked to Mayfield after his victory. His boxing career had been hardscrabble, with no givens or guarantees. Bored one day when he was 20, he had wandered into an old gym in San Francisco. He watched a few guys spar and was coaxed to get in the ring. He knew he could handle himself, having rumbled in the streets since an early age. He was told the other guy was like him, a boxing novice. Didn't seem so in the early going, as the guy popped Mayfield with numerous jabs. Growing impatient, Mayfield tore into his foe and battered him until the match was stopped. He was informed later that he had been lied to. The guy he had stopped was an amateur with a number of fights under his belt.

Inspired by how well he had done, Mayfield returned to the gym daily. He was told he had an annoying style. He considered boxing a hobby at the time, but ended up winning 54 of 59 amateur fights. Annoying with something else, obviously.

Mayfield captured the 2006 Golden Gloves in his home city. The naysayers were silenced, though they would return often. Mayfield ignored them. He turned professional at 24. His style was frenetic, awkward, and intense.

"The kid can knock you dead with one punch," trainer Virgil Hunter told me in 2010. "He can throw punches from odd angles and still knock guys out. Karim is strong."

Getting fights was difficult. Once an important boxing city, where heavyweight champions Bob Fitzsimmons, James J. Corbett, James J. Jeffries, Jack Johnson, Joe Louis, Ezzard Charles, and Rocky Marciano had drawn blood, San Francisco was now a mere afterthought. Mayfield was trying to change that but the odds were against him.

Six months after defeating Santana, Mayfield fought for the first time in his hometown. The venue was Kesar Pavilion a rock's throw away from the site of the famous Rocky Marciano vs. Don Cockell heavyweight championship fight held at Kezar Stadium in 1955. The Marciano fight drew a reported twenty-two thousand boxing fans. Mayfield fought in front of close to a thousand against one Sergio Joel De La Torre. Poor old De La Torre had maybe three people cheering him on that night, and they were all in his corner. Mayfield prevailed by a fifth-round stoppage.

Mayfield fought on ESPN in 2011, besting former champion Steve Forbes. His big chance came four months later, when he got a shot at the vacant NABO super lightweight belt against determined Patrick Lopez. Mayfield felt some nerves before the fight. He remembered the advice a very smart 10-year-old had given him before the Golden Gloves. "Don't let the fire consume you," said the youngster. "You'll be OK." Mayfield floored Lopez twice in round four. He battered his taller foe, winning the fight by unanimous decision. Mayfield was elated. "It was great to see my vision and dreams come true," Mayfield said after the fight. "I was leaving with the championship belt. It was amazing."

Seven months later, Mayfield was back on ESPN, this time defending his newly won crown against slick Raymond Serrano. The crouching Mayfield pursued Serrano throughout the fight. Serrano wanted to box, but was soon slugging with Mayfield. Bad decision. In round three Mayfield's Sunday punch (his right) put Serrano down. The fan favorite was up at six but woozy. Mayfield pounced. Serrano used his legs to avoid most of the incoming. Round four was competitive until Mayfield dipped a Serrano jab and let fly with a doozy of a right hand. The punch turned Serrano into Paul "The Punisher" Williams. He hung in the air for a millisecond, before collapsing to the canvas. The gutsy youngster beat the count but wobbled to the ropes. The chaos in his disorganized corner did nothing to help him. Serrano answered the bell to begin round five but was obviously out on his feet. Referee Eddie Claudio waved off the fight at 47 seconds into round five.

I pondered this as I drove through the historic Fillmore District, where Mayfield had grown up. He represents his neighborhood with great pride. I spotted the eatery and found a place to park. I got out of my car and started walking. The area was old and scarred, with empty buildings. The delicatessen was at the end of the street. One streetlight flickered behind me.

As I got closer, I spotted a number of guys milling out front. They eyed me suspiciously. Might have figured I wasn't from around there. They were right. I stopped and looked around. They came closer. No smiles. Only a few feet now. Just then I heard a noise from behind me. The gang stopped, one yelling, "It's Karim!" He had parked right behind me. Mayfield got out of his car smiling, his newly-won championship belt hanging over his shoulder.

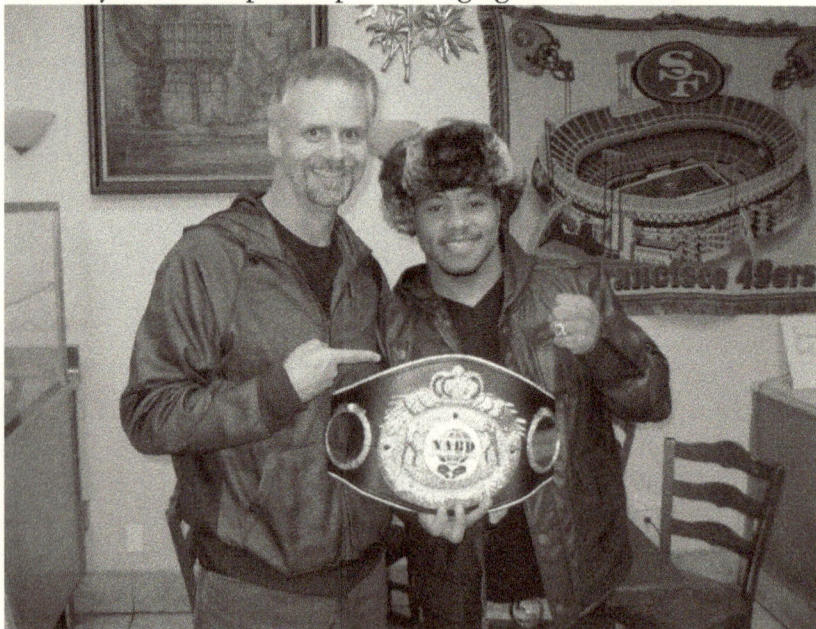

"Hey!" he said. "This is John, he's a writer, he's cool." I didn't feel very cool, but was glad he thought so. We went to eat and talk.

Later we were joined by Ken Watson, a boxing instructor. Nicknamed "Doc," and dressed in a white suit, Watson had known

Mayfield for years. "I always knew the kid had it in him," Watson said, his voice rhythmic like a cool jazz record. "He was so determined. It was just a matter of using his energies in the right way. As soon as he figured it out, he did it." I glanced at Mayfield who was listening intently. It was obvious that "Doc's" words, and the man, meant a lot to him. We chatted some more, interrupted occasionally by calls of "Hey Champ!"

After our meeting, I felt a certain pride for what Mayfield had accomplished. He had defied the odds, and now, was giving back to his community. I sat in my car and watched him shake hands with the same bunch of guys who were earlier dubious due to my presence. Now I was OK, because I knew the Champ.

Mixed Emotions

By Jerry Fitch

It will always puzzle a few people who know me, or at least know of me, when I tell them that I no longer follow boxing. After all, I began watching boxing in the late 1950s and started writing about it in 1969. As recently as a few years ago I was still offering articles for Boxing World Magazine. Of course I still continue to write books, however these are always of a historical nature. I consider myself a historian first and foremost these days.

Even more so it may seem strange that I once sat ringside rooting like any other fan of boxing. I enjoyed watching two warriors beating each other senseless. Personally I have been splattered by blood at ringside. I even had the occasion to spill some of my own blood and return the favor in the ring. It never occurred to me that someday I would feel totally differently about all of this.

I have met no less than sixty former and current champions and many contenders and non-contenders in my lifetime. I am proud to say that I met such greats as Jack Dempsey, Rocky Marciano, Joe Louis, Willie Pep, Archie Moore, Henry Armstrong, Ezzard Charles, Muhammad Ali and many more. Some like Jimmy Bivins, Jimmy McLarnin, Jersey Joe Walcott, Tony Zale, to name a few, became special friends for many years.

Appearing before fight fans promoting my books, or appearing on radio or television or even when being interviewed by newspaper reporters, sometimes the questions asked are sensitive and point blank. I was caught off guard a few times when someone would ask me, "Were any of the guys you met punch-drunk?" I admit I usually manage to sidestep these questions the best I can. I have always been protective of these men, feel no need to expose their flaws or infirmities before the public. I have to be honest some of the fighters I have met, interviewed, even became friends with have shown some of the effects of the ring. A few have had slurred speech, memory loss, or in worst cases some physical problems. Many times their family members would tell people that their husband or father or grandfather had Alzheimer's. Many of us of a certain age have witnessed firsthand family members who never once laced on a glove but suffer from dementia. It seems saying dementia or Alzheimer's sounded better than Pugilistic Dementia.

Most family members were prideful and didn't want to admit that boxing did that to their loved one.

However I have read accounts of fighter's wives and other people flat out condemning boxing and in some cases even calling for a ban. One prime example was a story in the *Plain Dealer* (Cleveland) on September 18, 1983, in the Reader's Column. Theresa B. Merritt, was the widow of former professional heavyweight, Dan Merritt, known as "Big Dan" during the 1940s. He had won the National Golden Gloves Heavyweight Championship and the Chicago Tribune Championship in 1938. He began boxing at age 16. According to his wife his life was shortened drastically by the damage done while he was fighting. His widow said, "I watched my husband's health decline due to brain damage to both sides of his temporal zone." She went on to say that when Dan died on January 24, 1980, "the doctor said it was from 'Pugilistic encephalopathy,' which means that his brains had been beaten out." The article was a lot longer but you get the picture. For the record Dan Merritt had a losing record and was knocked out fourteen times. He met many of the heavy hitters of his era including Curtis Sheppard, Elmer Ray, Lee Q Murray, and Lem Franklin.

Most cases never became part of any public record. I have made it a point never to give up their names. But some fighters have been out in the public where the general public can see these serious signs of dementia. One fighter in particular, the late Bobby "Schoolboy" Chacon was seen at many events, on videos and also had stories written about him. I am not revealing anything about Bobby that everyone doesn't already know. It was very sad to see what the ring had done to Bobby. In 1983 after his second fight with Boza Edwards, Bobby wrote to me in a postcard and told me he wanted to just have a couple more fights and then quit. He did continue to fight for a while but I suspect the damage had already been done.

There are many other tragic stories including that of the former boy champion and defensive wizard Wilfred Benitez. Locally there have been sad stories also like that of former heavyweight Terry Daniels, who once fought Joe Frazier for the heavyweight championship. Terry hung around way too long and now lives the kind of life nobody would want for a fighter or anyone else they know and love.

When I was deeply involved in boxing I actually did go to bat for the sport a number of times. There have always been advocates for banning it. Famous doctors have more than a few times come out in newspapers with information and recommendations about the negative side of boxing. I remember once where a world famous Neurosurgeon from Cleveland Metropolitan General Hospital conducted brain scans of several local Cleveland boxers. The tests were done in secrecy with the agreement given to all participants that their names would never be revealed to the public. To my knowledge the names have never been revealed. However the report from the doctor stated that all of the former and then current fighters had some damage and several had significant damage to their brains. In all my years of interviewing Cleveland area fighters I never once heard of anyone admitting to being part of that trial back then.

When I was defending boxing back in the day I would point out the numerous injuries in other sports. This is true, even more so these days. Professional football has had so many players hurt via concussions from blows to the head. And soccer also has come under fire. In some cases leagues are now banning younger players from heading the ball. So other sports do cause injuries but the focus on boxing of course is to hit your opponent as hard as possible in the head. I know it will never be totally safe, and I will not get on a soap box and call for a ban. But I no longer can defend the sport.

So these days I am strictly a boxing historian, I have been for a good number of years. I can safely say that most of the fighters I have met have been friendly and nice and it has been a very rewarding experience. I learned that many of these fighters, even the ones who had a brutal rough-and-tumble style in the ring, often were the most gentle, kind and some of the most talented men you would ever want to meet. Such fighters as Mickey Walker and Georgie Pace, to name a couple, took up painting. Others went on to work with the youth of their city helping many youngsters get off the street. Some very good trainers have evolved from the ranks of former boxers also. Some ex-fighters went into other surprising fields of work, often the exact opposite of boxing and what you would expect.

I engaged in a few amateur fights and sparred many times in the gym. Truthfully I was not that naive to think I couldn't possibly get hurt, perhaps even seriously. I was well aware that taking blows to the head was not a normal thing. But when you are young you feel differently about such matters. The combat of boxing is contagious.

When I watched fights as a young boy I had no clue permanent damage was happening before my eyes as I witnessed men getting cut and sometimes knocked out on our TV screen. I was not aware of the physical part of the whole thing, the life altering damage that more than likely was happening. Even when I first started covering boxing and sitting ringside I never thought much about the negative part of the sport. It was exciting and I thoroughly enjoyed it in those days.

Till this day I still admire the fact that unlike team sports boxing is so personal. It is one on one with another man, nobody can help you but yourself. No matter what your corner says, no matter how many people ringside yell out instructions, when the bell rings it is just the two of you. That is special and very unique to most sports.

During my lifetime I have either witnessed or read about several ring deaths. Benny Kid Paret, Davey Moore, Johnny Owens, Kim Duk-koo are just a few of the men who lost their lives from boxing during my years covering or watching boxing.

I believe the first time I seriously took notice of a fighter who obviously took too many punches and survived was when I saw a short story from the Associate Press on June 14, 1972. The story told of the plight of the former Light-heavyweight Champion Maxie Rosenbloom who was in his 60s and in a sanitarium minus his memories. After his lengthy career he had been a restaurant host and an actor who often played the role of a punch-drunk fighter. At the time of the article he was under the care of The Motion Picture and Television Fund. The article said physically he was fine for his age but he couldn't remember how great he had been, he couldn't remember his friends and had no clue he had been champion of the world. He died in March of 1976.

One of our more famous local fighters ended up in a nursing home in southern Ohio. One day his son told me that he had gotten a call from the nursing home and was asked to please come down there immediately because they had a serious situation. Sadly the former fighter had actually punched a nurse. When his son got there his dad muttered to him, "I heard the bell, I heard the bell." I will never forget that.

Just like many older adults, fighters sometimes don't show signs of the damage the ring has caused until years later. It normally doesn't happen overnight. Some men for whatever reason maintain their mental sharpness for most if not all of their lives. But I would say that is more the exception than the rule.

I don't ever want to appear as a hypocrite. I wrote and still write because I truly believe these ring warriors deserve to be remembered. I will never refer to these men as bums or stiffs just because they didn't maintain or even achieve greatness. It takes a lot of courage to step into the squared circle. Some men are not cut out for it and so they either quit altogether or quit during a fight without offering much effort. There are also many who fought for years, gave their all, but just didn't quite have the ability to achieve greater heights. And there are more than a few who were just unlucky. You know the ones, the guys who always seemed to be on the short end of split decision losses or hometown decisions. Like a lot of athletes fighters find it hard to quit, always thinking they will turn it around with one more fight. Most often that never happens. That part of sports, even more so in boxing, bothers me a lot. Quitting sooner than later does not happen as often as it should. Boxers need to be protected from themselves, and they need to be taken care of after they retire, not cast aside and forgotten.

Yes, I have mixed emotions now. I have no regrets that I was once very much involved in boxing. I was for a very long time. I really have no regrets for loving boxing as much as I did.

I don't feel bad about not covering or following boxing now. I have many fond memories of my time being involved in boxing and have met some remarkable people. Regardless of how I feel now, the past has been special and I enjoy telling the history of the fighters I met and the events I was able to attend.

I especially feel good knowing that the many fighters I have written about appreciated my efforts as did their families. I have always strived to give them their just due. Regardless of whether they were great or just so-so, I wanted to give them the credit they so richly deserved. I want them to never be forgotten. In my opinion there is no better reward than that.

The Trainer

By John J. Raspanti

I didn't meet him in the conventional way. Quite the contrary.

In 2011, trainer Virgil Hunter's top fighter, 2004 gold medalist Andre Ward, would be fighting heavily favored Mikkel Kessler in a matter of weeks.

I had arrived early at King's Gym in Oakland, CA, to interview Ward. This was our second interview. As we spoke, curious onlookers milled around the ring, situated near a back wall, occasionally glancing our way during the 30-minute interview. Ward was friendly, but intense, answering my questions with ease, since we'd met before.

I had written a number of articles about Ward's rise. I was convinced he was the real deal. His upcoming fight with WBA champion Kessler was expected to be the biggest yet of his promising professional career.

Kessler had lost once in 44 fights. That loss was to undefeated Welsh star, Joe Calzaghe. Kessler and his people didn't consider Ward much of a threat – more a joke, in all honesty. There was cockiness in Kessler's camp. Ward was just as confident, but not in a cocky way. He believed completely in himself.

We concluded the interview and shook hands. Ward was itching to get to work. As I watched him walk over to his team, I noticed a tall bald man watching him intently. His eyes took in everything. I recognized him as Virgil Hunter, Ward's smooth and articulate trainer. Ward had on his headgear and gloves and climbed into the ring. Music echoed around the gym. His sparring partner stood in the opposite corner, waiting on Ward, and the bell to ring.

I had asked Ward if I could watch him spar a few rounds. He had agreed. Ward's team had draped a tarp in front of the ring. They were worried someone could sneak in and record his sparring sessions. I had seen the tarp when I entered the gym. Ward and Hunter stood in the corner and talked. A few others stood by the tarp eyeing whoever walked nearby.

I pulled out my camera, checking to see if it was charged. I was planning on taking some pictures of the outside of the building. I heard a voice cut through the music. "No pictures!" I flinched and looked up. The music stopped. Everyone in the gym looked at me. I fought the notion of assuming the position - raising my hand in what I hoped was a reassuring way, and said, "No pictures. Don't worry."

I heard Hunter ask in an incredulous voice, "Who is that?" I assumed Ward told him I was a writer. Hunter looked at him and back at me. I felt like a burglar who had been caught in the act. Hunter glanced my way a few more times as Ward worked. I didn't dare move.

Hard to imagine that uncomfortable first meeting would lead to many pleasant conversations over the years. Our first interview took place a few months after Ward had taken care of Kessler. Things had changed since then. Ward was hot, and so was his trainer. At that point, I still wasn't sure what to expect, especially after that meeting in the gym.

We were to meet at a place called "Coffee with a Beat" located near Lake Merritt in downtown Oakland. I arrived early and went inside to look at the menu, and discovered that Hunter frequented the place often. There were a number of pictures of Hunter and Ward on the walls. I found out later that Ward, while training for the Olympics, would jog around the lake while Hunter waited at the "Beat." I liked the place. The building was old but filled with happy faces. They nodded at me. Very friendly. I nodded back. I was dressed like I thought a writer should be, with a backpack slung over my shoulder. The shirt I was wearing gave me away though. It had a picture of Jack Dempsey on it.

I waited outside for Hunter. He arrived promptly at our arranged time. He looked like a trainer, decked out in Everlast sweats, black shirt, and green cap. We locked eyes. I nodded, he smiled. I introduced myself, told him who I was writing for. Apparently, he was curious about me as well. We walked inside to order our coffee. As we waited, he peppered me with questions about websites and how long I had been writing.

We found a table outside and sat down. I had roughly twenty questions for Hunter. I quickly found out that boxing ran in his blood. "My grandfather was a fighter, and my father was a fighter," Hunter said. "My grandfather was a barnstormer throughout the south and my father was the all services champion. He never turned professional. My uncles boxed, so I was exposed to it at a very early age."

Hunter's uncle Lem taught him how to box. It was something expected. Everyone in Hunter's household talked boxing. I nodded and told Hunter about my family's background in boxing. Hunter also played college basketball and baseball. A full dance card. When he said he boxed, I assumed he meant professionally. His answer surprised me. "I boxed more or less along the gun-slinging route." said Hunter.

His answer conjured up a picture of a ring protected by guys with guns. Not totally crazy. Since its debut over 200 years ago, the Sweet Science has been filled with law breakers, loaded guns, and violence. They didn't call it the "Red District Sport" for nothing. He could likely tell by the look on my face that I was perplexed by his answer. Hunter set me straight.

"I can explain that to you," he said with a smile. "I was in the gym quite a bit, fought a lot of smokers (fights conducted under the auspices of a private, charitable club), but I didn't have much time. Basketball was my love of participation, boxing was my love of meditation. So you know, once I started slowing down in the participation, the meditation came forth."

Hunter grew up admiring Sugar Ray Robinson. Later it was former heavyweight champion, Larry Holmes. He's always been interested in styles and the mental aspect of the sport. I asked him who would have won if Holmes, who was once Muhammad Ali's sparring partner, and Ali had fought in a real fight. "Well, I think because Holmes was Ali's sparring partner for so many years, Ali was taxing him," Hunter said. "So then Ali would have won."

"Oh yeah," I interjected. "It was mental too."

"Yeah, but what I'm saying is that Ali beat Holmes a lot in sparring. Holmes beat up Ali once. Ali of course hadn't fought Joe Frazier yet in Manila, so that's when he (Holmes) broke it off. He knew he could hold his own with Ali, but it's questionable whether Holmes could have beat George Foreman or Joe Frazier." It felt like I was a student in a boxing class. Hunter was making me look at things from another angle. He said Robinson was great, but he wished he would have been more physical.

"I wonder why Basilio (Carmen) gave him such a hard time and Fullmer (Gene)," Hunter said. "He wasn't physically strong like they were. He was a strong boxer, but he wasn't a strong fighter. So they caused him quite a bit of problems." A couple of events paved the way for Hunter to become a boxing trainer. In the 1990s, he sparred with former heavyweight, John Tate, who was considering a comeback. Hunter was playing semi-pro basketball, not sure what he wanted to do.

Then his phone rang. His old trainer called and said he needed help with some kids. Hunter liked the work immediately. He worked under three experienced boxer trainers, learning the trade.

He learned different ways and styles--the jab, short punches, and infighting. He incorporated a slip-and-slide style his grandfather had shown him. Virgil Hunter had found his calling. I asked Hunter what he thinks makes a good trainer.

"The ability to observe," he said. "To shut your mouth and observe who you're training and allow them to show you what you're training." The mental side of boxing has always fascinated me. Hunter as well. He saw many instances of kids who seemed cavalier, but in the ring, they refused to lose. Focus is the key. Development and progress. Some fighters can ignore problems outside the ring, others can't. The ability to think is also paramount to Hunter. "I like a fighter to be able to adapt and adjust," Hunter said. "Because sometimes you can be very close-minded." I asked Hunter about talent versus a great attitude. His answer surprised me a little.

"You know, I've had kids like that (a great attitude) and I tell them what I can do for them," said Hunter. "I can train them to be very exceptional at taking care of themselves on the street. I'll give them a style that's conducive. As far as the ring is concerned, yes, they can compete. But they're not going to be a world champion. They won't be bad. But, you know, I can train them, and around their block they'll be a legend, but in the ring - it's always talent."

Hunter met Ward when the future two-division winner was nine years old. He noticed immediately that Ward had very strong observation skills. Hunter had Ward fighting pros at 15. Ward's talent and maturity were years ahead of his competitors. At this point during our discussion I reminded Hunter that he scolded me during Ward's workout.

He said, "Did I do that?" I nodded. He shook his head. For the next five years, I talked to Hunter as often as I could. Usually it was before and after one of Ward's fights. His insight was always uncanny and revealing. He'd always make time. By now, Ward was champion and Hunter had been named "Trainer of the Year." I'll never forget one time I watched Hunter and Ward from outside the ropes. I could feel the tension between them. Ward had been away from the ring for over a year. He was defending his title against Edwin Rodriguez. Hunter was talking a lot during the mitt work. His words weren't exactly complimentary.

After working together for twenty minutes, Hunter was smiling as Ward paced nearby. Hunter bounded down the ring steps and whispered to me, "He's ready." I nodded. Hunter then added, "When they get a little edgy, you know they're ready."

By this time, Hunter was doing color commentary during televised fights. His success had not changed him. Okay, perhaps his wardrobe changed. He had exchanged Everlast for Air Jordan.

We'd hug every time we got together. We'd talk boxing and family. I'd always conclude our get together by saying, "You remember when you yelled at me?" He'd shake his head and smile.

My Favorite Fighters

By Jerry Fitch

In my previous book titled *My Favorite Fights,* I wrote about various fights that for many reasons were my favorites during my lifetime. I did not list them by popularity or the fact they were necessarily all time great fights, rather that they were fights that were my favorites. I wrote about some fights that I actually saw ringside and also fights I viewed on live television, closed-circuit or film and video.

When I think about my favorite fighters I have to use that same format when picking them. There is no way I could have seen all of my favorites fight live obviously. I wasn't born until 1946. I will have to admit I have had a lot of favorites over the years so it is not easy to narrow it down to just a handful.

In no particular order I will have to say that some of my favorites are probably favorites of a lot of fans. How can any true blue boxing aficionado not pick such a great as **Joe Louis** and some others from back then. In the case of Joe Louis I have watched many of his fights extensively. Thankfully a lot of Joe's fights are available for all of us to see. Even though I met Joe Louis a couple times I was never fortunate enough to really get to know him. But his great ability as a fighter was amazing and his 25 title defenses record breaking. I truly feel as far as heavyweights go nobody was a better all around puncher. He had it all, a jab that could knock people down, a big right hand and outstanding left hook. To his critics who say he shuffled and was slow, well I have to say he was not slow when it came to hurting and finishing off even the best of fighters. And his footwork was very good, he did not have a lot of wasted motion.

I have been fortunate to meet a lot of former greats because I started following boxing at a very young age and also was able to travel extensively. I was always curious about the earlier greats in boxing and what they looked like in action. Most of the time footage has been available and I have been able to see what made them such good, even great fighters. Joe Louis died on April 12, 1981. I have visited his grave in Arlington National Cemetery.

One of my other favorites will always be **Jimmy McLarnin**. Having read about him for years and seen some of his fights on 16mm film, I knew he was very special as a fighter. I eventually was able to meet him in 1975 and discovered two things. Not only was he one of the all-time great welterweights, becoming a two-time champion, he also fought thirteen men who held a world title and defeated twelve of them. Jimmy's most famous series of fights was with another all-time outstanding fighter, Barney Ross. Their three fights were classics during a special time in boxing when there were so many excellent fighters around. Jimmy also quit the ring on a high note, having defeated Tony Canzoneri and Lou Ambers in his last two bouts. Although money could have tempted him to make a comeback he never considered it. As far as being a good friend, I can only speak for myself. He was genuine in his friendship. I wrote about my more than ten year friendship with him in my book *50 Years of Fights, Fighters and Friendships*. Jimmy lived to be almost 97 years old, passing on October 28, 2004.

When I was really young one of the first fighters I actually took notice of was **Jersey Joe Walcott**. I saw his contorted face from the first Marciano fight on the cover of a sports magazine. It caught my attention. Years later in 1964 I was able to meet Jersey Joe and throughout the years we met up several times and had some great conversations both in person and through correspondence. Joe and I were together in Washington, D.C., Los Angeles, New York and Toronto. As a fighter he was remarkable in many ways. When he became the oldest man to win the heavyweight title in 1951, he did it with a single punch. Sadly for him when he lost the title to Rocky Marciano in 1952, it too was by a single punch. Joe's style was unlike anything I had ever seen. His shuffle, his footwork, how he walked away from an opponent and then turned and launched a right hand was special. He had power in both hands. His struggles earlier in his career, his never-say-quit attitude endured him to the boxing public. He won the title on his fifth try at it. That says it all about the man. Jersey Joe passed on February 25, 1994.

After **Rocky Marciano** took the title away from Jersey Joe he was the main focus of many fans. I remember seeing him on television shows and his face was plastered on many magazines. I was honored to finally meet him in 1964 at the Cleveland Arena. But I never really had a friendship with him, it just wasn't meant to be. I have, however, watched several of his fights on film and video. Marciano's first fight with Jersey Joe Walcott is without a doubt one of the greatest heavyweight championship fights. I have probably watched that fight more times than any other over the years. I also love watching other Marciano fights, especially the Archie Moore battle. I will not get into the constant argument about whether Rocky fought old men, over the hill fighters and whether he should or shouldn't be considered an all time great. He came along when he did and certainly was one of the best ever conditioned fighters. He was a huge puncher and a hero to Italian-Americans everywhere. His 49-0 mark with 43 knockouts was and is very special. It will always be everyone's choice or opinion how Rocky ranks among the all-time greats. It is an argument I have elected to ignore. Sadly Rocky Marciano died young in a plane crash on August 31, 1969.

I think the first heavyweight champ I really followed from the start of his career to the finish had to be **Floyd Patterson**. Even though I didn't get to meet him and see him fight in person until 1971, I was fortunate to meet up with him several times after that in New York, Los Angeles, and Toronto. Floyd without a doubt was one of the all-time great gentlemen of boxing. Always humble, always a class act. As far as his career goes, to me he had moments of greatness and also moments of utter disappointment. The first part of his career saw him win an Olympic Gold in 1952 as a middleweight. Later he became the youngest man to win the heavyweight title when he knocked out Archie Moore in 1956. From there on he lost and won back (also a first) the heavyweight title from Ingo Johansson.

my sincere best
wishes for a
healthy and happy
life.
Floyd Patterson

Needless to say most people will remember Floyd's two humiliating defeats to Sonny Liston, both in the first round in 1962 and 1963. It seemed at the time it was over for Floyd, he would never again be a factor in the heavyweight boxing scene. But we all were wrong.

To me the second half of Floyd's career was much more rewarding for many reasons. Floyd fought Muhammad Ali twice during that time and lost both. The first fight in 1965 he had a bad back, the second in 1972, a badly damaged eye finished him off in what would be Floyd's last fight. I am not saying Floyd could have ever defeated Muhammad Ali but a least in the second match he accounted himself quite nicely until the stoppage.

Also in the second half of his career he had quality wins over Eddie Machen and George Chuvalo in what was *The Ring* magazine's Fight of the Year in 1965. He cold-cocked Henry Cooper in four in 1966, had two questionable fights with Jerry Quarry in 1967, one being called a draw, the other a majority decision loss. He then lost an outrageous decision to Jimmy Ellis for the World Boxing Association World Heavyweight Title in 1968 in Stockholm, Sweden. The majority of people felt he deserved the decision. I have watched that fight several times and agree. Later Floyd won a decision over the always tough Oscar Bonavena in 1972. When Floyd retired after his second fight with Ali his record stood at 55-8-1, with 40 KOs. He trained fighters and became the New York Boxing Commissioner and sadly died at the age of 71 on May 11, 2006. He was always special to me. When he was young I truly believe he had the fastest hands of any fighter I had ever seen. Archie Moore always said Muhammad Ali was the fastest heavyweight he ever saw but Floyd Patterson had the fastest hands. He should know.

Joey Giardello was another fighter I took notice of after seeing him on the cover of a magazine. I don't remember the exact title on the front of the magazine but it was something like "Trouble is a guy named Joey." Basically the story was about how middleweight Joey Giardello had gotten into trouble and served time. Later he had a couple controversial decisions, one in fact he took to court to win. He had apparently defeated Billy Graham on December 19, 1952 by split decision. After the fight boxing Commissioners Robert Christenberry and CB Powell altered one of the judges cards to change the verdict to a win for Graham. The original cards had referee Ray Miller scoring it 5-4-1 for Giardello and judge Joe Agnello having it 6-4 for Joey. The other judge, Joe Shortell scored it 7-3 for Graham. The Commissioners then changed Agnello's card. Joey took it all the way to the New York Supreme Court and the court reversed the reversal, once again giving Joey his rightful decision win.

Joey had a storied career. When it was all over he had won 101 fights and had defeated Dick Tiger on December 7, 1963 in Atlantic City to win the middleweight championship. The list of who he fought during his career was filled with all the top fighters. He never ducked anyone.

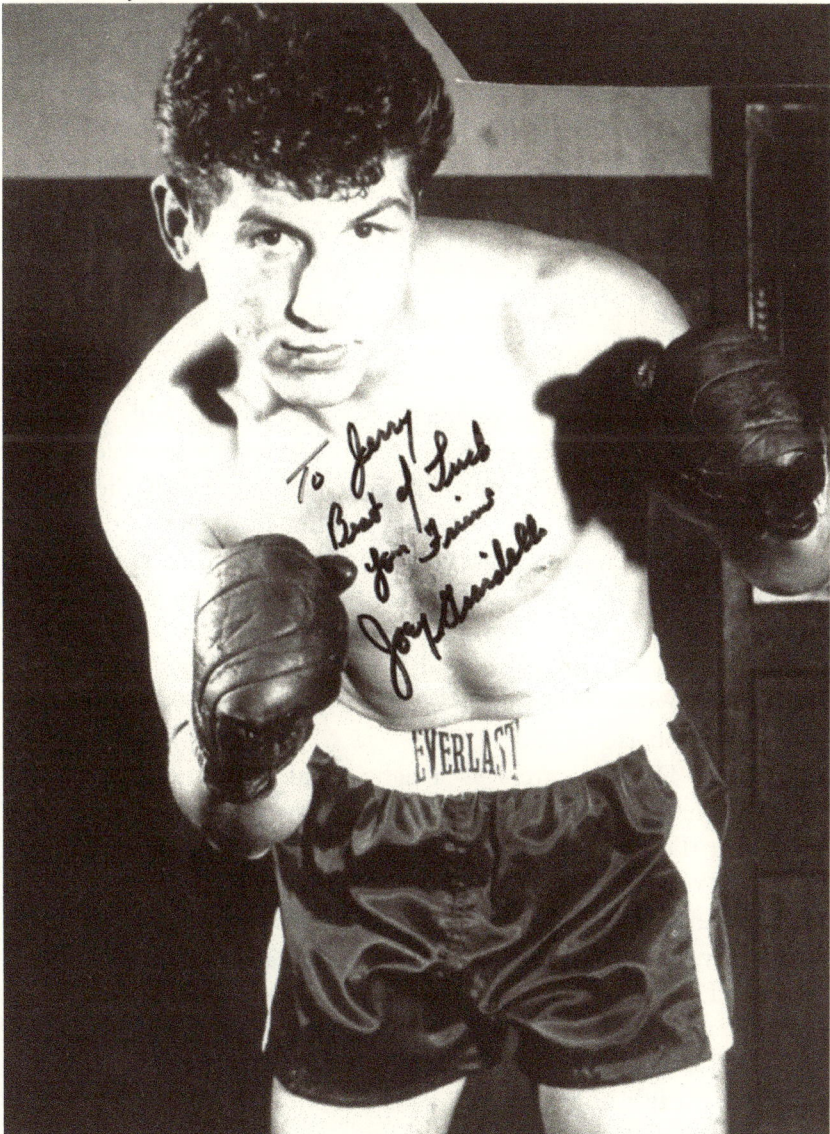

Even in retirement Joey Giardello had other controversies. The movie "The Hurricane" falsely portrayed him as getting an unfair decision over Rubin "Hurricane" Carter in 1964. This was not the way the fight actually went. Joey had skillfully won a unanimous decision. Joey later sued the movie makers and won an out of court settlement.

I read a lot of articles about Joey and was fortunate to meet him once and also exchange letters with him a few times. He was always friendly and very generous when it came time to autograph photos. But what will always be my fondest memories of Joey is the fact I was able to see him fight live three different times at the Cleveland Arena, once in 1959 against Dick Tiger and twice in 1964 against Rocky Rivero in grueling non-title fights. He won them all, as a matter of fact, Joey was 7-0 in Cleveland during his career and called Cleveland his "lucky town." It is said Joey hung out in Cleveland's Little Italy when he was in town. He had the support of the local Italian crowd, that I am sure of. I consider myself lucky to have been able to see him live, meet him and write about him. There is no way I could keep him off my favorites list. We lost Joey on September 4, 2008.

Roberto Duran was a fighter who first caught my interest for all the wrong reasons. When he won the title in 1972 from Ken Buchanan of Scotland, the ending in the 13th round really bothered me at the time. It appeared Ken got fouled with a low blow after the bell. The referee is as much at fault as anyone. Whether it was an accident or intentional the fact Johnny LoBianco didn't even acknowledge it happened was a puzzlement for sure. Most people ringside saw it and fight footage showed it clearly. The fight was stopped and as most followers of Roberto Duran will say, he was way ahead on all scorecards and perhaps might have stopped the champion anyway. It certainly caught my attention and spiked my interest in Roberto Duran.

Roberto Duran's career as a lightweight to me ranks up there with the very best. The feeling of most fight fans seems to be that he is near the top with names like Joe Gans, Benny Leonard, and perhaps Ike Williams. His fights with Esteban DeJesus, the first man to defeat Duran were classics. Of course his first fight with Sugar Ray Leonard in June of 1980 was special. At the time I thought Leonard would win this fight without much trouble as Duran was moving up in weight. However the Montreal battle was a classic and Roberto fought an awe-inspiring fight to win the welterweight title unanimously.

After this fight, which was yet another high point for Duran, he and Leonard were involved in the famous "No Mas" fight later in 1980. I don't think we will ever know what really happened or what was going through Duran's mind when he suddenly told the referee he wanted no more, he had quit in the 8th round. I sat down with Roberto in 1981, in his hotel room in Cleveland prior to his comeback fight with Nino Gonzalez. I did ask him what occurred in the second Leonard fight. To say he was vague would be a huge understatement. Between the translation and his own words it was hard to tell what really must have troubled him back then. I am sorry he didn't give me something more in what otherwise was a classic interview. I wrote about the interview in a chapter of my 2013 book, *50 Years of Fights, Fighters and Friendships*.

I was fortunate to see Roberto Duran fight in person twice. And I got to experience him working out at our gym, The Parma Boxing Club, prior to his comeback fight with Gonzalez in 1981. He drew big crowds everyday he worked out and it was obvious he was a huge fan favorite. His career in the last years had a lot of ups and downs and surprises like his win over Davey Moore to garner the WBA Junior Middleweight title in 1983. I don't believe anyone felt at the time he would put up such a strong effort as his fifteen round loss to Marvin Hagler in November of 1983 in quest of the World Middleweight Title. You could never tell with Roberto.

Joe Frazier will always be a favorite of mine. So much of my early writing career in boxing included Joe Frazier. I had followed him long before I ever attempted to write or cover a fight. From his Olympic Gold to his steady climb up the heavyweight ladder I was intrigued with this man and his style of fighting. As he made his way into the world rankings the names Charley Polite, Memphis Al Jones, Billy Daniels, Oscar Bonavena, Eddie Machen, Doug Jones and eventually George Chuvalo appeared in the win column for the man who would become widely known as "Smokin Joe Frazier."

Boxing has always had classic matches that seem to roll off the tongue of fans who have closely followed the sport or at least know the history of it. Who doesn't know of Dempsey-Tunney, Louis-Schmeling, Louis-Conn, Zale-Graziano, Pep-Saddler, Marciano-Walcott, just to name a few of the classic matches of men who fought against each other more than once. Of course you have to add the Frazier-Ali (or Ali-Frazier) trilogy to that list.

When I was writing for London's *Boxing News* during the period of 1973-77, I wrote about Ali and Frazier more than a few times. The weekly had a Reader's Column where fans could write in and voice their opinions, often about what we columnists wrote in a previous issue. I will always remember how one or two readers "attacked" me because I said something negative about Muhammad Ali and seemed to be pulling for Joe Frazier. One time a guy even called me a racist because I was not giving Ali high praise in his upcoming fight with England's Joe Bugner. It was rather silly needless to say because I have always been totally color blind when it comes to fighters. Followers of my work know I not only write about fighters of color, I have been blessed to have more than a few as longtime friends. Still it showed how much Muhammad Ali was beloved by the majority of fight fans. Yet it was ludicrous to think I was racist when I was writing about Ali and Frazier.

I am not a fool, I am well aware of the impact Muhammad Ali had in boxing and even worldwide for many reasons. A guy like Ali comes along once in a lifetime. I would be remiss not to consider him one of the top heavyweight fighters of all time. We can argue till the end of time whether Ali is better than Joe Louis or Jack Johnson or Jack Dempsey or whoever you want to choose. Muhammad Ali was great no doubt. The fact I don't have him as one of my favorites in this chapter has nothing to do with his ability or impact. Muhammad Ali was a huge part of my writing days when I was very active with several magazines. I covered his fight with Chuck Wepner at the Richfield Coliseum in 1975. I witnessed all of his fights. Ali was very nice to me in our encounters, once he even made a cassette tape message for me for a friend in New Zealand. That happened in 1975, prior to his third fight with Joe Frazier.

I just happened to be a huge Joe Frazier fan. I am not going to apologize for the fact I was pulling for Frazier in all three Ali fights. There was something about Joe, his blue collar style, his grit and toughness. One of my friends who lived in New Zealand referred to him as a "bulldog" in the ring. I loved watching him and was saddened when he was destroyed by George Foreman. Joe only knew one way to fight, coming forward and bobbing and weaving, getting in close, launching his left hooks. Even in his second fight with Foreman where he tried to box a bit, it just wasn't Smokin Joe. Styles make fights and Joe Frazier and Muhammad Ali were made for each other. The fights with George Foreman showed that Joe Frazier was made to order for Big George. I would rather remember the Joe Frazier who whipped Ali in 1971, gave him two other classic efforts, beat Jerry Quarry twice, Jimmy Ellis twice and clobbered Bob Foster. He may not have been as great as Muhammad Ali and some other all time greats, but he was special. I am glad I got to meet him in person but even happier that I witnessed a lot of his career. He will always be one of my favorite fighters. Joe left this good earth on November 7, 2011. Muhammad Ali followed him on June 3, 2016.

Emile Griffith is another fighter I followed a lot. So much of my boxing life, as I like to call it, occurred when Emile was fighting. It would be hard to pick which fights I loved the best. Of course his three fight series with Cuba's Benny Paret ended on a sad note. Emile was trained and managed by the team of Gil Clancy and Howie Albert. On the way up the ladder Emile had met a lot of good fighters such as Randy Sandy, Gaspar Ortega, Denny Moyer, Florentino Fernandez and Luis Rodriguez. Eventually Emile got his title shot and won the welterweight title from Benny Paret with a knockout in round thirteen in 1961. He lost it back to Benny via a decision that same year and then regained it in 1962, when he stopped Paret in round twelve after landing countless punches before the referee, Ruby Goldstein stepped in and stopped the fight. Paret slumped to the canvas and was taken out of the ring on a stretcher. Benny Paret died ten days later without ever regaining consciousness. A lot has been written about that fight and events leading up to it and the effect it had on Griffith for the rest of his life. The fight was witnessed by countless people on national television. It was a sad time for boxing and foes of the sport clamoured for a ban at the time.

Some of the best fights of that era came about when Emile and Griffith and Luis Rodriguez, an Angelo Dundee trained fighter, played ping- pong with the title. Rodriguez won it from Emile on March 21, 1963, Emile won it back on June 8, 1963 and then they met in a rubber match for the title on June 12, 1964, with Griffith coming away the winner to retain his title. All three bouts were close and depending on who you asked some felt Luis Rodriguez deserved a better fate. They were that evenly matched.

Emile defended his title a few times against the likes of Brian Curvis, Jose Stable and Manuel Gonzalez, before taking on Dick Tiger for the World Middleweight Title on April 25, 1966 and coming away the winner.

Emile defended his latest title three times against Dick Tiger and twice against Joey Archer, a crafty fighter who gave Griffith all he could handle. Then once again Emile was involved in another classic trilogy. This time it was with Italy's Nino Benvenuti where in 1967 and 1968, Emile lost the middleweight title, won it back from Nino and eventually lost the third bout to the handsome Italian, all three bouts by decision.

Emile dropped down in weight to challenge Cuban Jose Napoles for the welterweight title in 1969, but lost a clear decision to Napoles. Who knows if they had fought earlier what might have happened. In 1969 Jose Napoles was on top of his game and Emile wasn't.

I witnessed the start of Emile Griffith's last great run in boxing. On January 28, 1970, promoter Don Elbaum managed to sign Griffith to meet his own charge Doyle Baird at the Cleveland Arena. After losing the title to Benvenuti, Emile had gone 5-3. He seemed to be treading water. Doyle Baird had shown great promise, holding Nino Benvenuti to a draw in 1968 (most thought Doyle won) in Akron and defeating Don Fullmer by a tight decision in 1969 at the Cleveland Arena. I knew coming into the fight Baird would be hard pressed to defeat Griffith. And he didn't no matter what his fans might have thought. Griffith won a decision over Baird and it really wasn't that close.

From that point on Emile won nine more fights including bouts with Carlos Marks, Tom Bogs, Dick Tiger, Nate Collins, and Ernie Lopez. This launched him into a title fight with Carlos Monzon in 1971. It was sad to watch as the much bigger and stronger Monzon manhandled Emile before the fight was halted in the 14th round.

Emile still had some bullets in his gun however and came back with several big wins including defeating Armando Muniz, Ernie

Lopez again and twice getting the best of Joe DeNucci. In 1973, Carlos Monzon graciously gave Emile another crack at the middleweight title. To his credit, Emile lasted the 15-round distance.

The rest of his career Emile Griffith had a lot of ups and downs. He was giving his all right till the end. As a matter of fact in 1976 he received one more title shot, losing a 15-round decision to Eckart Dagge on September 18, 1976 in Berlin. It was for the WBC Junior Middleweight Title.

Emile ended up with a great career no matter how you look at it. He was a three-time welterweight champion and two-time middleweight king. I feel very fortunate to have watched so many of his fights and finally meet him in 1970 when he fought in Cleveland.

Emile left us on July 23, 2013.

Sugar Ray Robinson is most always on historians and fans lists as one of the greatest, if not the greatest pound-for-pound fighters ever. I can't argue with that and yet I can also see where some may not always agree. Sugar Ray Robinson always seemed to be in the news when I was young. Before there was a Muhammad Ali there were guys like Kid Gavilan and Sugar Ray who not only had great fighting ability but were very flamboyant and just as big outside of the ring as they were in it. Ray had businesses in Harlem, New York and when he traveled to Europe he had his pink Cadillac with him. He drew crowds everywhere he went.

Sugar Ray seemed destined to be a great fighter even in his amateur days. He had it all when it came to the skills needed for boxing; speed, footwork, punching power and the ability to take a good punch.

Many books have been written about Sugar Ray and perhaps there may be more. I finally met him near the end of his life although I was not able to spend much time with him. Because of this and knowing that some very gifted writers had already written about his life, I have refrained from attempting to write such a book. However I considered it a great honor at the time to actually meet him and still do. My trips to California were always rewarding and he was someone I had always hoped to meet one day.

The Ray Robinson story could take up many pages of this chapter if I had elected to do so. In my opinion Robinson was at his greatest as a welterweight. One of my biggest disappointments viewing films of his career is that some of his classic matches at that weight are not available. His two fights with Kid Gavilan are a perfect example. They would have been special to see.

Sugar Ray's career had many memorable fights, not the least of which was his six fight series against Jake LaMotta, who he eventually won the middleweight title from in 1951. His career in the middleweight division certainly was historic because he managed to lose his crown several times and also retire and make a comeback. By the time his career ended he had defeated Jake LaMotta, Randy Turpin, Bobo Olson, Gene Fullmer and Carmen Basilio to win the middleweight title five times.

Sadly like so many fighters Sugar Ray hung around too long. By the time he finally quit for good he had participated in over 200 fights and had won 175 of them with 110 knockouts. He was admired by many future boxers including Muhammad Ali and eventually Ray Leonard who was named after Sugar Ray Robinson. Till this day in most boxing forums even the youngest fans know who he was. It is not a stretch when he is listed as the greatest pound- for-pound! Sugar Ray died on April 12, 1989.

Larry Holmes probably will always be controversial it seems because he was outspoken and as they say rubbed people the wrong way at times. I think when judging a fighter you must first and foremost look at his ability and accomplishments, not what he may have said in the heat of the battle. I know many people for whatever reason do not like others for things that were said or done and they take it personally. I have been guilty of that also. I try to be open-minded when it comes to talking about fighters as I think that is the only fair and honest way to discuss them and how they rank amongst their peers.

I also feel that Larry Holmes should not have to be defended by me or anyone else. He was one of the best heavyweight champions in my mind. The length of his heavyweight reign and number of defenses rank right up there behind Joe Louis. He had a lot of great qualities including one of the best left jabs ever and a fighting heart. As far as his chin goes all you have to do is watch the replay of the thunderous right hand Earnie Shavers landed on him in the seventh round in their second meeting on September 28, 1979. Everyone knows the power of Earnie Shavers and what he could do to any opponent if he landed one of his big punches. The right that landed on Larry was not a glancing blow, it was a straight on bomb. When it happened I was sure Earnie Shavers had won the heavyweight championship. But Larry got up rather quickly and I couldn't believe what I had witnessed. If anyone had doubts about the makeup of Larry Holmes it surely was dispelled that moment. He would go on to stop Earnie in the 11th round to retain his championship and end the dreams of Earnie Shavers.

Larry's trainer, the late Richie Giachetti, is given a lot of credit for the rise of Larry Holmes. It is not my intention to say otherwise. But I can say this about Richie. He and I did not like each other and I might even say Richie really didn't like me. I am not going to discuss the reasons because at this stage of my life it is not important and Richie is not around to add his two-cents on the issue. I will however say that Richie was quoted more than once as saying "I said Larry Holmes would not amount to anything as a fighter." That is so far from the truth it is ridiculous. In fact it is just the opposite.

On November 28, 1973 Don King put on his first major boxing show when he scheduled one of his fighters Jeff "Candy Slim" Merritt in a match against Ron Stander in a ten round main event at the Cleveland Arena. On the undercard Larry Holmes was matched up with Kevin Isaac. This was Holmes' seventh professional fight. I had not ever seen Larry in action but had heard good things about him from his sparring with a lot of excellent fighters, Muhammad Ali among them.

In round three of this fight Larry got careless and Isaac floored him. I think everyone was stunned because of the pre-fight build up of Holmes. I will admit I hadn't expected it. But Larry got up quickly, got on his bike and before you knew it he landed a picture perfect left-right combination and floored Isaac. It was all over as the fight was stopped as a TKO win for Larry.

After the show I was talking to Lew Eskin. Lew was a referee on the card, and I had known him for several years. Lew had given me my first writing assignment in 1969 and my first feature in 1971. Lew was running *Boxing Illustrated* at the time. Years before that he worked at *The Ring* magazine. Several of us were sitting around and I casually mentioned to Lew that I felt Larry Holmes had the potential to possibly become heavyweight champ someday. I based that on his size and composure and that great left hand. I was certainly impressed with him that night and realize now that making that statement probably seemed odd, especially since Larry only had seven pro fights. But I said it, I know I did and I am not claiming to be any fortune teller and I normally didn't try to predict the future. I do know 100% I never said Larry would never amount to anything!

Larry ticked off a lot of people, especially the Italian-American community when he made a statement in frustration. After losing to Michael Spinks he got into a heated exchange with reporters and said something like "Marciano couldn't carry my jockstrap." The discussion came up because he had come close to equalling Marciano's record of 49-0 as a heavyweight champion.

Larry's career was excellent and I suppose some people only remember his fight with Muhammad Ali in 1980. It should have never taken place. Ali should have retired before then but we all know how tough it is for fighters to quit. Holmes was looked at as the bad guy because of the one-sided nature of the fight. Larry was winning easily when the fight was stopped. Ali was a shadow of his former self that night. Then there was the Mike Tyson fight in 1988 where Larry was stopped for the first and only time in his career. That was not a good fight for Larry at that stage of his career for sure.

Finishing up 69-6 with 44 knockouts is pretty impressive. His championship reign was one of the best. How anyone ranks him I will leave up to them. I know he was good, perhaps one of the best ever and certainly he is one of my favorites.

Jimmy Bivins is a man who most followers of my writing know I rank as one of the best fighters ever. He was my friend for more than forty years. Winning 86 fights, defeating 8 world champions, countless other great fighters such as Charley Burley and Lloyd Marshall speaks volumes. He was rated in the top ten most of the time from 1940 until 1953 and is in several Hall of Fames. Over the years I have written features on him in *The Ring* magazine, *Boxing Illustrated* and *Boxing News* (London), among other publications. I wrote a book on him in 2011 and did a follow up to that in another chapter in this book. He will always be one of my favorites and nothing will ever change that. Jimmy left us on July 4, 2012 at age 92.

Crazy Nights And Fights At StubHub Center

By John J. Raspanti

I'll never forget the roar of the crowd when heavy underdog Alfredo Angulo connected with a crunching left hook to the jaw of Erislandy Lara on the night of June 8, 2013.

The sound exploded like a bomb above the lights of StubHub Center in Carson, CA. Situated six rows from the ring in the media section, I literally jumped out of my seat. It will always be a mystery to me why the relatively small venue has hosted so many boxing classics. I've often wondered if the outside arena, somewhat reminiscent of the gladiator days in Rome, brings out the extreme warrior in fighters. There's no quit, no give. Blood spills but nobody seems to care.

A similar burst of enthusiasm had occurred in the co-main when "The Riverside Rocky," Josesito Lopez, faced off against tough Argentinian Marcos Maidana. The year before, I witnessed Lopez upset Victor Ortiz at Staples Center in Los Angeles. Nobody gave Lopez much of a chance when the fight was announced. His record showed four losses in 33 fights. Not bad, but nothing to write home about. The biggest name on his resume was Jessie Vargas, who edged Lopez by split decision in Las Vegas, NV. two years before.

Ortiz was coming off a knockout loss to world champion Floyd Mayweather. The fight was controversial. Though winning, Mayweather was being pushed a little. All hell broke loose in round four. A frustrated Ortiz head-butted Mayweather in the mouth. He immediately felt bad, apologizing and hugging an already annoyed Mayweather over and over. Before Ortiz could say, "Love ya, Man!" Mayweather knocked him on his ass. Ortiz had forgotten the classic adage "Protect yourself at all times." Mayweather made him pay.

Before the fight, Ortiz talked of redemption. Supposedly, he'd be fighting Mexican superstar Saul "Canelo" Alvarez if he defeated Lopez. "The Riverside Rocky" felt disrespected. "They (Golden Boy Promotions) could have waited to make the announcement," he said. I agreed with him. If anything, Lopez entered the fight even more motivated. He delivered, living up to his nickname.

Ortiz did well in the early rounds, clocking Lopez with left hands. Lopez absorbed them and battled back. Southpaw Ortiz boxed more in round three, but was caught by two rights. Ortiz appeared to stun Lopez with a combination. Ortiz did even better in round four. Another combination stopped Lopez in his tracks. Lopez followed, but did little else. Ortiz peppered him with shots. Lopez did better in round five. A beautiful left-right landed clean. Ortiz went back to boxing in round six. His educated jab was on point. He seemed to be in control, but with Ortiz, consistency can be a problem.

Round seven had the crowd on its feet. As Lopez languished on the ropes, Ortiz ripped off a sharp combination. He looked at Lopez like he expected him to fall. Lopez checked him with a right. The blow sent Ortiz a step back. Lopez dropped his hands and motioned for Ortiz to continue. Lopez told me after the fight that he "wanted to show him (Ortiz) I was here to fight." No doubt Ortiz got the message. Lopez was walking though Ortiz's punches as the crowd chanted his name. Ortiz connected with a three-punch combination in round eight. No matter, the skinny-but-brave Lopez kept coming.

Lopez was puffy, but fought on. Ortiz hurt him with a huge left in round nine. Lopez shook off the blow and returned fire. Near the end of the round, Lopez hurt Ortiz with a sweeping right. Seconds after the round ended, Ortiz' trainer stopped the fight. Ortiz spit blood and shook his head. His jaw was broken, but quitting is never accepted in boxing. Unless you're Roberto Duran. As Ortiz exited the ring to catcalls, blood streamed from his mouth as Lopez reveled in victory.

Three months later, Lopez stepped in for Ortiz and was stopped by the much bigger Alvarez. Lopez took some time off and returned nine months later to face Maidana at StubHub. Lopez would need to be the matador to the bullish Maidana. He had most of the sellout crowd in his corner. And in the early going, he boxed smartly, resisting the urge to get into a firefight. The match changed when Maidana started to dig to the body. As his fans roared, the wiry Lopez stunned Maidana with a big uppercut in round three, but was soon on the receiving end of a booming right.

Lopez had a good round five, but Maidana upped the ante in round six, applying intense pressure. The bodywork had done the job. Lopez couldn't make a dent in him. An overhand right sent Lopez to his knees. He got up, but soon reeled sideways until the referee waved the fight off. I can remember writing as the sound reverberated around me like waves.

The Lara vs. Angulo bout was a classic match-up of boxer versus slugger. Lara had the faster feet and hands. A combination wobbled Angulo. The crowd favorite went to the body in round two. Lara used his big edge in athleticism in round three. His movement kept Angulo off-balance. The slugger needed Lara to stop moving so he could set his feet and punch. Lara wasn't cooperating. The fight changed in round four. Angulo, who had been whiffing with his power punches, connected with a crushing left hook. Lara was down, and the roar was probably heard a mile way. Lara beat the count and was quickly back in control, only to be floored again in round nine. The fight was eventually stopped in round 10 due to a broken orbital bone in Angulo's left eye.

The crowd was so rowdy that night that two of them started yelling at one particular boxing writer--me. It didn't start that way. They had ventured to the railing, separating the media from the fans to yell at promoter Eddie Hearn. Check that. They didn't really yell. They bellowed. At the top of their lungs. E D D I E!!!! Over and over. I was trying to write and their screechy voices were making me crazy. Imagine a violin in heat. After hearing "Eddie" squealed for the sixth or seventh time, I turned around and said, "Hey! Can you guys knock it off?"

They did, for about five seconds. I think I shocked them. One tried to climb over the railing, but was stopped by security. I went back to writing my report. Paid them no mind. After I finished, I unplugged my computer and packed up my stuff. The big-mouth guys were gone. Or so I thought. As I walked toward the ring, the same security guy who had intercepted one of them saddled over to me. He said, "Maybe you should go another way. Those guys look like they're waiting for you." He pointed behind me. I could see the loudmouths watching us. I smiled and shook my head. "I could go with you," he said. "Nah," I replied. I heard them yell as I walked away. I figured if they rushed me in the parking lot, I'd crown them with my computer. They didn't show.

A year later, I was back at StubHub to witness the brawl between Robert Guerrero and Yoshihiro Kamegai. The fight looked like it would be over in the opening stanza when the heavily-favored Guerrero abused Kamegai's face with wicked combinations. Kamegai took the blows and asked for more. Guerrero was hitting Kamegai with everything but the ring post. In round three, a stinging left hook knocked Kamegai into the ropes. He was hurt, but instead of going down, he pounded his chest and let out a Tarzan-like scream. The crowd screamed with him.

Though battered, he wouldn't quit. He opened up a cut over Guerrero's left eye in round six. There was no way Guerrero, nicknamed "The Ghost," would disappear.

Although deeply religious, the soft-spoken Guerrero loves to mix it up. He staggered Kamegai with a wicked uppercut in round 10 and was a little wobbly himself during the next heat. The 12th and final round ended in an all-out brawl, with no semblance of technique. Guerrero and Kamegai walked to the center of the ring and went toe-to-toe as the fans screamed themselves hoarse. At the bell, the boxers smiled and embraced as some folks threw money into the ring.

A few months later, I was back at StubHub to watch the coronation of Gennady Golovkin. Before the bout began, Golovkin did a victory lap around the arena. Every boxing fan was standing and screaming. I wondered how that made his opponent, Marco Antonio Rubio, feel. The fight hadn't even started, and here was Golovkin waving at the crowd as the celebrated champion. No matter, Golovkin jolted Rubio with a left hook in round two, and put him away with another hook off the top of the head. Golovkin took a bow in the center of the ring as roughly nine thousand fans serenaded him. The guy hits like a mule and fights like a calculating assassin. I've talked to Golovkin a number of times. Nice guy. It would have been interesting to have seen him fight the top fighters when he was in his 20s. He was 30 when he arrived in America. His prime was short-lived.

Unfortunately, I wasn't on hand to witness the wars between Israel Vasquez and Rafael Marquez, Brandon Rios and Mike Alvarado, Ruslan Providnikov and Timothy Bradley when the place was called the Home Depot Center.

No matter, even from the comfort of my own living room, I'll always hear the crowd.

Potpourri

By Jerry Fitch

Not all of my stories have ended up in a fight report or even in a feature article or book. Some of my stories are just fragments of events or afterthoughts from the days when I spent a lot of time attending fights and covering boxing.

Doyle Baird an Akron, Ohio middleweight was a good fighter. Maybe not great but very good. I saw many of his fights in person in Cleveland and Akron. He always came to fight. However one memory of Doyle was a brief encounter I had one late night in February of 1970. It was after Doyle had taken out Cleveland's Earl "Sugar Cane" Johnson in two rounds at the Cleveland Arena. The fight itself was exciting while it lasted. On the way home I pulled up at a traffic light at the corner of East 36th and Euclid Avenue, just west of the Cleveland Arena. I was driving a big old Buick with a 455 cubic inch engine in it. I looked over and there was Doyle Baird in a dark car, either an Oldsmobile or Cadillac. All I remember is that it was a big car. I rolled down the window and yelled over to him. I barely knew Doyle but I managed to joke with him and challenged him to a race. At the time I suppose I didn't think he would take me up on it. Yet he did and next thing you know we were roaring down Euclid Avenue at high speed without a care in the world. Fortunately it was during the days when Cleveland's streets were not busy late at night and we never saw another car and certainly not a police car. Who won? Depends on who you ask.

Willie Williams was a local lightweight who at best could be called an opponent. Promoter Don Elbaum used guys like him to fill out his fight cards. Willie was a southpaw who seemed to move around the ring like he was doing some sort of jitterbug dance. Willie was always announced as "Wonderful" Willie Williams. He wasn't really all that wonderful and his final career record was 10-39-5 and he was stopped 24 times. He was a character and the one lasting memory I have of him is that he normally entered the ring wearing calf length dress socks, sometimes the Argyle style.

Ernie Terrell the 6'6" heavyweight had a decent career winning 46 out of 55 bouts. He even held a piece of the heavyweight title when he won the vacant WBA version over Eddie Machen in 1965. Of course everyone remembers his fight with Muhammad Ali in 1967 when he refused to call Ali by his Muslim name. Calling him Cassius or Cassius Clay infuriated Ali and he dealt out some severe punishment to Ernie throughout the bout, constantly asking Terrell what was his name. Terrell never gave in to the plea no matter how many times he was asked. It was a terrible fight that left him battered. It was ugly to watch.

My favorite memory of Ernie Terrell came after his fight with Buffalo's Vic Brown on April 28, 1971 in Cleveland. Ernie mauled his way to a unanimous victory. The main event on that card featured Cleveland Williams giving a boxing lesson to local upstart Ted Gullick, flooring him in the 10th round and winning a majority decision.

After we left the Cleveland Arena that night a few of my friends decided to stop at the Versailles Motor Inn at East 29th and Euclid Avenue. Several of the out of town fighters were staying there. I joined my friends and we went into the lounge to have a few beverages. A local band was playing. We relaxed and listened to the music for a while. A short time later Ernie Terrell walked in and went up to the band. He spoke briefly with the group and the next thing we knew he joined them for several songs. As a singer he was quite good. When he was finished, we waved at him and he came over to our table. We told him how much we enjoyed his singing and that is when I learned Ernie had quite a musical background and that his sister Jean Terrell had replaced Diana Ross with the Supremes. After his retirement from the ring Ernie continued to perform with his group the Heavyweights. He even had a gig in Las Vegas for a while and appeared on Johnny Carson's Tonight Show.

Randall Tex Cobb was a heavyweight whose career was quite colorful. He had some big victories including wins over Earnie Shavers and Bernardo Mercado. He also lost very close fights to Ken Norton and Michael Dokes. Perhaps he is most famous or infamous for taking 15 rounds of punishment from Larry Holmes on November 26, 1982, while challenging for the WBC Heavyweight Title. Personally I felt some good came out of that fight because it convinced Howard Cossell to give up announcing. That's just my opinion.

While spending time in California in October of 1985, part of my visit was to attend The World Boxing Hall of Fame dinner and induction ceremony. I was a member of The Board of Directors of that organization at that time.

During this California trip I almost got to see Tex Cobb fight live. I say almost because as it turned out it never happened. On October 29, 1985, several of my friends, including George Luckman, John Peterson and Gary Ballin made a last minute decision to head to Reseda, California because we heard that Tex Cobb was fighting that night against a guy named Dee Collier. Normally when we went to fights we bought our tickets in advance. This time we just went on a whim. We figured why not, we hadn't seen Cobb fight live before, so off we went.

The Reseda Country Club was not a very big place as we soon found out. We got to the venue late figuring we'd at least get to see the main event, which was the Cobb-Collier fight. The guy at the ticket window quickly told us the place was sold out. So we stood outside the Country Club planning our next move. Just then we heard a lot of roaring from inside the building and before we knew it people were beginning to file out. We asked one guy what had happened and he said, "Hell, Cobb got knocked out in the first round!"

Because Tex Cobb had a reputation for being rugged and had stood up to Earnie Shavers big punches, in addition to taking all that Larry Holmes could offer, some people were very suspicious of the ending to the Collier fight. There were rumblings of a fix and Sports Illustrated even published something suggesting Cobb took a dive. He had never been stopped before and never again after this fight. Cobb maintained he didn't do anything illegal and later sued Sports Illustrated and won.

Aaron Eastling and the low crawl. Aaron Eastling was a journeyman heavyweight from St. Paul, Minnesota who fought professionally during the years 1966 - 1970. His final record of 21-14-2 is a bit deceiving because most of his wins were against lower tier fighters and his losses were when he was matched up with the elite fighters of the heavyweight ranks such as Jerry Quarry, Ken Norton and even George Foreman.

My recollections of Eastling come from two local bouts, one in Cleveland and the other in Akron, Ohio in 1970. Eastling first fought locally against George Foreman on April 29, 1970, at the

Cleveland Arena. Later he was matched with Ted Gullick at the Akron Armory on September 14th. At the time Gullick was considered a topnotch heavyweight. Both fights were disasters for Eastling. Foreman stopped him in round four, while Gullick turned the trick in two.

My special memories from those two fights are for a different reason. In the second fight it appeared Eastling was intimidated by Ted Gullick before the fight even started. At least that is the way it looked from my viewpoint.

The Foreman fight was a whole different memory. Yes, this was the first and only time I was able to see George Foreman fight live. But what happened during the fight is what has stuck with me all these years.

The Foreman fight found Eastling knocked down once in the first round, once in the second round and then three times in the fourth round before the fight was stopped. However, what happened after one of the knockdowns is what I remember most of all fifty years later. Aaron Eastling was on the floor and he appeared to be trying to make an exit from the ring by crawling out under the ropes. Some may have thought he was just disorientated at the time from the battering he had absorbed. However I remember Don Elbaum the promoter running toward the ring yelling at Eastling to get back in the ring. It was quite comical at the time.

The Stig was a local sports-writer whose real name was Dennis Lustig. Dennis worked for the *Plain Dealer* in Cleveland for 20 years. He was known affectionately by his co-workers as "The Stig." Today, with political correctness, Dennis would be known as a little person. He was only 3 feet 8 inches tall. Back then, some of his fellow writers called him "The Dwarf."

During his career he mostly covered high school and college sports. He would go anywhere, anytime to seek out a story. He loved being a sports-writer and even though he sometimes was the brunt of jokes it never stopped him from doing what he loved. He was known by many of the major players in the sports world. It was said when teams came to town often their most famous players would ask how Dennis was doing.

Dennis eventually did some coverage of boxing during the later years of his career. He came to our gym and my friends and I fed him tips about who would be fighting locally or coming to train at our gym. We introduced him to fighters who he would then interview and write about for the *Plain Dealer*. Sometimes we would get frustrated because he would make minor mistakes about what weight division a certain fighter fought in. But he was always enthusiastic about writing about sports.

The one odd moment that comes to mind most about Dennis was the night my friend Don Myers and I and a couple friends were heading to Cleveland Public Auditorium, also known as Cleveland Public Hall, to watch a closed-circuit viewing of one of Muhammad Ali's fights. Dennis Lustig never drove so he asked us if he could tag along and of course we said yes.

Somehow we ended up a lot further away from Public Hall than we had hoped for. We also were running a little late. As we hustled down Ontario Avenue to get to the Lakeside Avenue entrance of Public Hall, Dennis Lustig was having a hard time keeping up. He finally asked my friend Don if he could carry him till we got to the entrance. Don didn't hesitate and boosted him up on his shoulders.

This is where things got a little weird to say the least. Some guys were walking near us and seemed to think it was wrong for Don to be carrying Dennis that way. I have no clue what was wrong with what we were doing but they started yelling, "Hey (expletive) put that little man down, put that little man down." They were creating quite a scene and we could tell Dennis was scared and kept asking Don Myers in a squeaky, panicky voice to put him down. Needless to say Don finally did. That seemed to pacify the strangers who were making such a fuss over the situation. It can safely be said these men were into their cups so to speak!

Sadly Dennis Lustig died at age 40 on November 25, 1984 from an apparent heart attack. An article the next day by the Plain Dealer's Bob Dolgan was titled "Long Live The Stig."

Frankie "Chee Chee" Wallace was born Franki Angelora in Campobasso, Molice, Italy on January 17, 1911. His parents came to Cleveland when Frankie was 6 years old. Frankie was a Golden Gloves champion in 1930 and was said to have had over 100 amateur fights with only 5 losses. He fought in the pros both as a featherweight and lightweight from 1930 to 1941. In 1931 until 1933 his name appeared now and then in the top ten rankings in the featherweight division and in 1937, he hit the top ten in the lightweight division. When his career was all said and done he had lost far more than he had won. However a closer examination shows he met most of the best fighters in the world during his career, some two or three times. His record is dotted with the names Bob Montgomery, Tony Canzoneri, Lou Ambers, Jack Kid

Berg, Kid Chocolate and Sugar Ray Robinson. He had career wins over Freddie Miller and Frankie Klick.

The funniest story I ever heard about Frankie Wallace was during one of his bouts with the great Lou Ambers. In the 6th round he had been holding his own when he suddenly quit. Afterwards a reporter asked him why he quit when he was doing so well and without hesitation Frankie told the reporter, "I had to go to the bathroom."

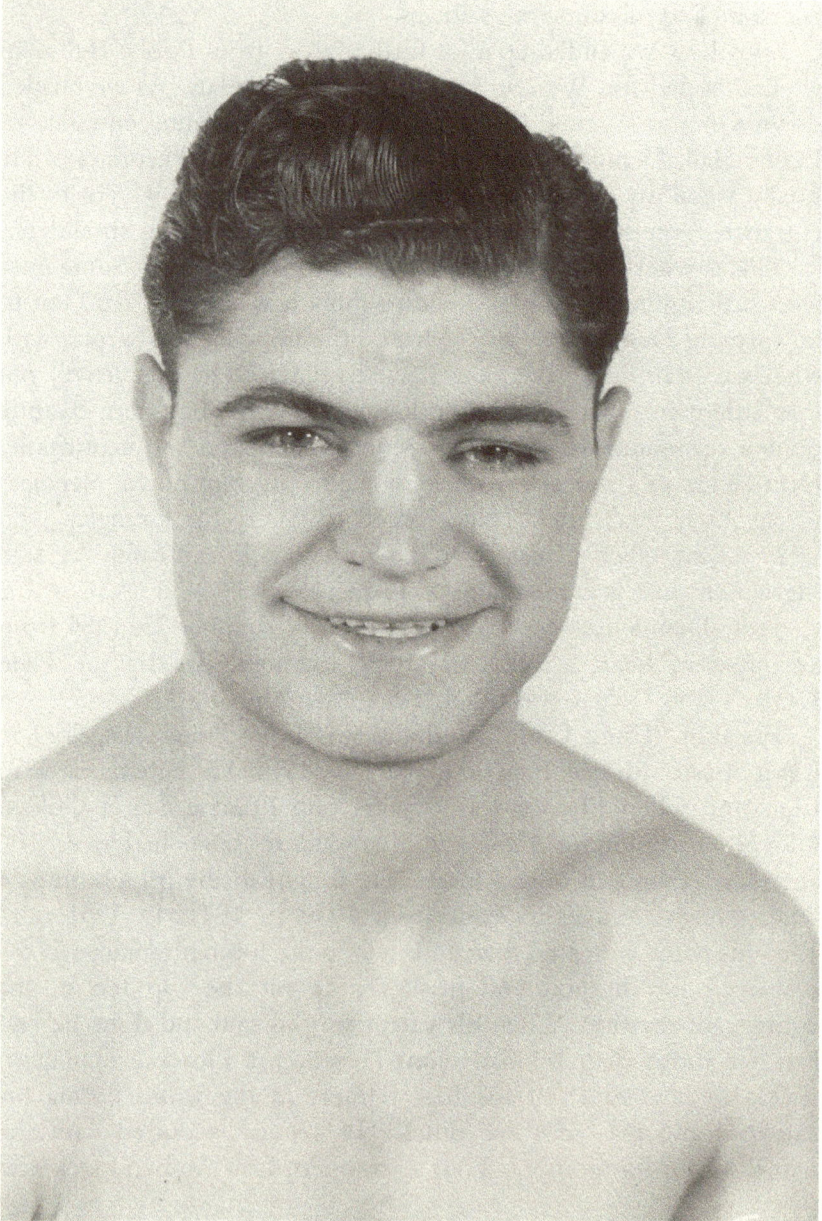

Landmarks And Live Boxing In Carson City, NV

By John J. Raspanti

"Hey Dad," I said in from the back seat of our car in July 1972. "There's boxing history around here." I saw his eyes light up in the rearview mirror. He was smiling.

"Around here" was Reno, NV. My family and I were visiting the "Biggest Little City in the World" from Southern California. At 13, I was bored with the idea of spending time there until I realized the city was where an epic fight took place in 1910. I read about it in a copy of *The Legendary Champions* by Ring Lardner that devoted an entire chapter to "The Fight of the Century" between champion Jack Johnson, and former champion James J. Jeffries.

We checked into our hotel and quickly went to the casino. Yes, the young me could gamble and never get questioned, perhaps due to the wispy stash above my upper lip. I figured you had to have attitude as well. I rarely smiled, except at the cocktail waitresses. After collecting a couple of drinks for Dad and Grampa, and no jackpots, I watched Dad play the slots. He didn't play just one at a time, more like four. He always bet the maximum amount, winning more than losing. He did it with flair, barely resembling the cool and calm guy I knew at home. Grampa was nearby applying his own particular style to the machines. He didn't play multiple machines like Dad. He played one at a time. After he pulled the lever, he'd look away. I asked, "Why don't you watch"? Grampa, who like my father, always did things his own way, looked at me earnestly. "Because, I don't like to see how close I come to winning," he replied.

I watched him play for a while, peeking at the symbols while he looked away. I admired his discipline. Mom walked by and asked if I had won anything. I shook my head. She hadn't either and was already bored. Grandma though, playing the penny machines, was winning like crazy. "She always wins," said Mom, shaking her head. This was true. And so did Dad. I heard a bell and stared at the red lights flashing above his machines, signifying he'd hit more jackpots. I figured now was a good time to hit him up on the boxing history I had mentioned earlier. He looked very happy.

"Dad," I said over the commotion. "Johnson and Jeffries had their big fight somewhere around here." He nodded, "I have an idea where," he said. Now I smiled. The fact that he knew the location didn't surprise me. He was master of finding out things. He loved doing that.

The next day Dad, Grampa and I hit the road. Dad pulled out of the parking lot like he knew exactly where he was going. I found out quickly he did. Within minutes, we arrived about four blocks from downtown, in an area of small industrial buildings. Dad turned right, made a U-turn, and parked at the corner as I spotted the plaque and let out a squeal. Grampa looked at me like I was nuts.

"Here?" I said looking at Dad and the plaque. He nodded, "Yep!" I jumped out of the car to get a better look at the plaque. It was silver and blue and had some scratching's on it. Still, I could easily read the inscription.

On this site on July 4, 1910, Reno hosted "The Fight of the Century," a heavyweight championship boxing match between John Arthur "Jack" Johnson, the African American title holder, and James J. "Jim" Jeffries, a former champion seeking to regain the title he had vacated in 1904. Jeffries had refereed a previous championship bout between Marvin Hart and Jack Root at this site on July 3, 1905, but the promotion of the ex-champion as "The Great White Hope" focused worldwide attention on his 1910 contest with the talented Johnson, known as the "Galveston Giant." Gamblers had their money on Jeffries, but Johnson easily handled his opponent and Jeffries trainers called the fight in the fifteenth round to save their man from the disgrace of a knockout. Organized by famed promoter Tex Rickard, they brought over 30,000 fans to Reno, some 22,000 of whom packed the arena here on the day of the fight.

It dawned on me that we had missed the anniversary by three days. I turned and looked at the corner lot. It was wide and substantial. A wood fence covered the entire area from the outside. It was certainly big enough to hold a ring that once held legends. It was hot this day, just like it was in 1910. I had read that the first bell rang at 2:10 pm. I asked Dad what time it was.

"A little after one," he said. I heard Grampa say, "I was a year old in 1910." I closed my eyes and tried to hear the crowd. I imagined the ring beyond the fence. The fight itself had not been memorable, other than the significance. Jeffries had his moments, but Johnson took his time and picked him apart.

I imagine that people driving by probably wondered what the skinny little boy on the corner was staring at. But to me, just to be here was special, and it was only the beginning.

Back in the car, Dad said casually, "There's some fights in Carson City later today." My eyes widened. I had been bugging him to take me to a live show for years. He'd nod and smile and say nothing. I asked who was fighting. He said a bunch of amateurs and old-pro Freddie Little. I had heard of Little. Luckily, I just happened to have my *Ring Encyclopedia* with me.

Little was a former champion with an impressive record of 50 wins and six losses. I felt my heart beat faster, then I thought of something else. Dad and Grandpa were talking. I could see we were driving away from downtown Reno.

"Hey, Dad!" I said. "You said Carson City, right?" Dad said yes. Grampa turned in the front seat and looked back at me.

"There was a championship fight that took place in Carson City," I said. I could see Dad's eyes in the rearview mirror.

"Who fought?" he asked.

"James J. Corbett and Bob Fitzsimmons," I replied, not missing a beat. Grampa chuckled and said, "When was that?"

"1897."

They both laughed. I knew that Dad loved it that I was so into boxing. He had been, as well, back in his hometown of Chicago, Ill. I think, more than anything else, I surprised him with my knowledge. The subject was endlessly fascinating to me, especially the old-time fighters. The drive from Reno to Carson City took about 45 minutes. Along the way, Dad told us the fights started at 4. The place was the Tahoe-Carson Speedway.

I had no idea where in Carson City the fight between Corbett and Fitzsimmons had taken place. Dad told me we'd find the local library and ask them. Libraries always have someone who knows these things. The librarian didn't bat an eye. She answered so quickly it was like she had been waiting for us.

Again, like the Johnson-Jeffries location, we were close. A plaque similar to the one in Reno sat near the curb directly in front of the Carson City police department and local post office. I scampered out of the car and read what it said out loud.

On March 17, 1897, at an arena located on this site, Carson City played host to Nevada's first world championship prizefight, a fourteen-round thriller in which the reigning heavyweight titlist, James J. "Gentleman Jim" Corbett, was dethroned by Robert Fitzsimmons. The Nevada Legislature had only recently legalized prizefighting and the match became the object of scathing criticism from the press and pulpit of other states, but fight fans by the thousands came in. Promoter Dan Stuart put on a clean show and demonstrated that boxing need not be brutal or crooked. Other states were soon to liberalize their own prizefight laws and the sport began to assume a degree of respectability it had not enjoyed in the past. In later years, Nevada was to be the scene of several other world championship fights.

The area was roughly two blocks long. If I had had my other book, I would have compared locations from then and now (I did just that 35 years later) Across the street were old homes with neglected lawns. It was hard to imagine a ring there, but I assumed it had to be in the huge parking lot. Corbett had always been interesting to me, beginning with the enjoyable and highly fictionized movie based on his life, *Gentleman Jim*, starring Errol Flynn.

"Come on," said Dad, "Let's hit the slots and get something to eat before the fights." The fights. I was finally going to see some boxing in person. What I didn't know then was our seats, if you call them that, would be located in an unusual place.

Fueled up and ready to go, we were soon back on the road. It didn't take us long to get there. I knew we must be getting close when Dad turned down a narrow roadway called Race Track Road. I can remember thinking some spectacular arena awaited us. Not really. What I saw was enormous race track. A ring with a spotlight over it sat in the center. My heart beat faster.

Bleachers were spread out in strategic locations. They appeared to be half-full with boxing fans. I could see what looked like a makeshift parking lot in front of us. Dad didn't go there. He pulled off the road and parked. We got out of the car and started walking towards the track.

Dad said, "Let's watch the fights from there."

There was the mouth at the bottom of the mountain. Grampa, the only one of us with a hat on to shield the sun, said "There?"

Dad nodded. I looked at the spot and back at the ring. The vantage point wasn't bad. We could see the ring clearly. It wasn't the nosebleed section. We found something resembling comfort on the mountain and settled in. Amateur fights kicked off the card. We were roughly 100 feet from the ring. The fights were good. The small crowd was really into it. Grampa as well. He'd pick the fighter he thought would win, based on body language He was mostly right. The one he got wrong surprised everyone.

The guy's name was Peter Wisecarver. He came into the ring dressed entirely in gold, waving to the crowd. His long blonde locks completed the look. All he needed was a surfboard. Dad filled us in on who he was. Wisecarver was considered something of a hotshot. He had Olympic dreams. The trials were coming up, and Wisecarver was fighting to stay sharp. Every pore of his being seemed to flow with confidence. He looked like a movie star.

His opponent, one Jean Mateo, climbed into the ring after Wisecarver. Nobody seemed to notice. His robe, unlike Wisecarver's gold one, was dirty brown and needed a good wash. His trunks were white with a stain in the front. His boxing shoes were red. At least they looked clean. He didn't smile like the golden one or acknowledge the crowd. He sat on a stool in his corner, staring straight ahead. It looked like his left leg was twitching. Grampa said, "Well, this one won't last long." He was right about that, but wrong about who would prevail. Wisecarver did well in the opening minutes of the fight, pounding Mateo's body with heavy shots. The blows made a thudding sound when they landed. The crowd loved it. Mateo ducked and backpeddled. He wasn't fighting back. Not a very promising start. Was he looking for a comfortable place to go down?

Then, he exploded. A long-overhand right from downtown Carson landed squarely on the golden one's chin. Down he went on his gold trunks. The small crowd roared in shock and disbelief. Wisecarver got up quickly, but seconds later was down again. I could see blood on his face. Wisecarver wobbled to the ropes and waited, like an inmate on death row. The killer was coming. Another overhand right hand deposited him seconds later. The bell rang ending the round.

"This fight is already over!" said Dad.

"That other guy hits hard," said Grampa.

"Or Pete has a weak chin," replied Dad. I said nothing, watching Wisecarver's corner feverishly work him over. The Olympic hopeful slumped on his stool, the fight beaten out of him. Still, when the bell rang, he bravely stood up. The referee shook his head. The fight was over.

"Wow," said Dad.

I watched Wisecarver exit the ring. Ten minutes before, he reeked of supreme confidence and acclaim. Now he needed help walking. The crowd ignored him. In the ring, the victor bowed and nodded. I felt sorry for Wisecarver.

It came near time for the main event to start. Dad had disappeared, returning shortly with a poster of the night's fights. I asked where he found it. He shrugged. The white and red poster was torn in a few places, with the face of Freddie Little dominating most of it. I knew exactly where it would go in my room.

I had read up on Little while Grampa and Dad gambled. The guy was a real pro. A former champion with a heavy punch. Little was 36, desperate for one more title shot. He had captured the WBA and WBC super-welterweight world title by defeating Stanley Hayward in Las Vegas. Back then, the super welterweight belt wasn't as respected as it is now. So Little, though a talented fighter, flew under the boxing radar. He made three successful defenses of his title, none in the United States. He lost his belt in 1970 to Carmelo Bossi in Italy. Many said he was robbed.

Little had won five straight matches since losing his title. The sun went down, but the huge spotlight highlighted the ring in a dramatic way. Dad, Grampa and I stood and stretched as Little, with a purposeful stride, made his way to the squared circle. His opponent, Billy Walker, was already in the ring. They both looked ready to go.

The fight was a barnburner. The unknown Walker stood toe-toe with Little and exchanged. Little got the better of it, but Walker hung tough. Until he didn't. After six rounds of intense action, the referee, after a quick discussion with Walker's corner, stopped the fight. It came as a surprise to everyone, including Little, and unleashed the boo-birds.

Fights over, we got up quickly and walked to the car. Little, tired of waiting for another shot at a title, retired a few months later. I glanced back up at the ring one more time as the spotlight dimmed. But the memory of that special day will always burn bright.

Keeping In Touch

By Jerry Fitch

In my days of being very active in many facets of boxing I was fortunate to travel to a lot of events, see a lot of fights and meet a lot of fighters. As I have mentioned before some of those encounters were brief and went no further than a one time meeting. Others lasted much longer.

The best part of boxing for me has always been getting to know former fighters and often carry on a correspondence with them. Many lasted a long time, others just a few years. Most of those friendships were during the time that no one had a computer. I wrote dozens of letters on some days, some to friends and others to former fighters as far away as New Zealand, Singapore and also various places in Europe.

I didn't keep every letter or postcard I received but I have managed to hang on to a decent amount of them. I stored them away in a box and have rarely looked at them as the years have slipped by. During the time of isolation because of Covid-19 I have found myself reading books and correspondence that I have not looked at for years. Most of the fighters I knew back then are long gone. I thought I would share some of my memories of those friendships from those days when many of us used to keep in touch.

Jersey Joe Walcott was the first champion I ever met. When I met him in the spring of 1964 at a fight between Joey Giardello and Rocky Rivero, I asked him if I could write to him. He said sure, "You can write me care of City Hall Camden, New Jersey." One day while playing softball with some friends I remarked that I had met former World Heavyweight Champion, Jersey Joe Walcott and that I planned to write a letter to him. None of us had any experience trying to communicate with famous people at that time so my buddies scoffed at my effort. I believe one of them said that I would never hear from him, even laughed when he said it. In spite of that I did write Jersey Joe a letter.

One day an envelope arrived and it contained a beautiful 8 x 10 photograph of Jersey Joe with the championship belt on, personally autographed to me. He also sent a nice letter thanking me for my letter, telling me he enjoyed my comments and that if I was ever in New Jersey to look him up. Naturally I had to show my friends the next time we got together. They were impressed. Little did I know at the time but Jersey Joe would be the first of many fighters with whom I would eventually correspond. It was a much simpler time, there were no computers or cell phones so we either would handwrite or type out letters to each other and often did not hear back for weeks, even months.

As the years went on I managed to see Jersey Joe again, first in Washington, D.C. and then later in Los Angeles. The most memorable encounter during those years happened in 1979 when the then Rochester Boxing Association asked me if I could get Jersey Joe to attend their annual dinner and receive their "Integrity Award". So I wrote Jersey Joe and he assured me if he wasn't booked for anything else he would be honored to come.

His letter was short and to the point. "Dear Jerry, I am in receipt of your letter dated May 21, 1979, requesting my presence at the dinner to be held in Rochester honoring Jimmy McLarnin and myself with the "Integrity Award" on April 19, 1980. I am looking forward to and hoping to be present at this dinner. Enclosed you will find the photograph of myself autographed to Terry Nick in England. I wish to thank you for everything you have done for me in the past." Sincerely, Jersey Joe Walcott, Athletic Commissioner.

The dinner wasn't scheduled until April 19, 1980, so there was a lot of time for me to worry about whether he would live up to his promise. As a matter of fact as 1979 went along someone started a rumor that Jersey Joe wasn't going to be able to make the dinner and was booked somewhere else.

As I have said there were no computers back then so everything went the slow snail mail route. If this happened today surely the communication would have been better. I did try to call Jersey Joe but never reached him. So I sent off another letter to him. As always he got back to me with a letter of his own. On December 6, 1979 he wrote to me with the following letter. "Dear Jerry, This will acknowledge receipt of your letter of November 19, 1979 regarding the Rochester Boxing Association Dinner scheduled for April 19, 1980. As a friend and gentleman I would like you to know that I gave my word that I would be present for the affair on April 19, 1980, and barring any unforeseen circumstances, I intend to be present. I have set the date aside on my calendar based upon our previous conversation and look forward to sharing some light moments with you and many friends in Rochester." The letter went on to say "As you may know there are demands made upon me as a person, as a Commissioner of Athletics, and as a State Director of

Special Projects. However, when a firm commitment is made by me, it will be kept, irrespective of comments and communications sent to you by other people. Without belaboring the point, suffice it to say, no firm commitment was made by me for attendance at the dinner alluded to in your letter. Thank you for your concern and I look forward to seeing you, your family and friends on April 19, 1980." He signed it Very truly yours, Jersey Joe Walcott, Athletic Commissioner.

Jersey Joe did attend the dinner along with my other invitee Jimmy McLarnin. He was a big hit and he and Jimmy Bivins had a lot of fun talking over old times. Jersey Joe was always a gentleman and treated me well. I admired him a lot. Our friendship lasted from 1964 until the late 80s.

George Pace held the NBA Bantamweight Title briefly in 1939. George came to Cleveland at an early age and like so many got his start in the local Golden Gloves. After some early failures he eventually won the City Golden Gloves as a bantamweight in 1933. He qualified for the National AAU in Boston but during training broke his left hand and couldn't compete. The hand would bother him for the rest of his career. George finished with a fine amateur record winning 63 out of 71 fights. George turned pro in 1934 and overall was rather successful defeating such men as Angelo Callura, Indian Quintana, Katsumi Morioka, Baby Yack, Henry Hook and Johnny Gaudes.

In 1939 his record stood at 19-2 and he was ranked near the top of the bantamweight rankings. Champion Sixto Escobar was having weight problems and refused to defend his title against George. Because George had defeated several men who had defeated the champion the National Boxing Association proclaimed George champion on November 2, 1939. Former Featherweight Champion Johnny Kilbane and great Hall of Fame ballplayer Tris Speaker, who was on the boxing commission, presented George with the certificate proclaiming him champion.

George tried for universal recognition when he met New York State Champion Lou Salica over fifteen rounds in Toronto on March 4, 1940. The fight ended in a draw. They were rematched on September 24, 1940 in New York and Salica won a 15-round decision to gain the title.

During WWII George served honorably in the United States Army in Europe. He decided to end his career in 1943 and go on with his life. His final tally was 32-12-2. He came back to Cleveland and stayed active, following the local boxing scene.

George had numerous health issues throughout his life and in later years would spend his winters in Arizona. He had severe asthma and other lung issues which often put him in the VA Hospital in Cleveland and Phoenix. He had a talent for watercolor paintings and would present them to fellow patients and staff at the hospitals. He was a man of faith and often painted religious scenes.

George and I actually first met at a local boxing dinner and hit it off right away. He and I would get together occasionally but would spend even more time on the telephone. When he spent winters in Arizona we would mostly write letters mixed in with a phone call now and then. He was a good friend and I enjoyed our years together. I learned a lot about faith and perseverance from this good man.

For some reason I have kept a stack of letters from George Pace. However one of his more interesting letters was dated March 14, 1978. George, although he had many trips to the doctor and the hospital, even while in Arizona, managed to be very active in the local Veterans of Foreign Wars chapters both in Cleveland and Arizona. He also managed to take in a few fights while in Phoenix and never failed to tell me his thoughts on the fights and fighters. In his letter of March 14th he spoke of watching a fighter named Jerry Schoolboy Cheetam fight and also had watched Edgar Bad News Wallace in a fight against David Love.

For a man who had so many health issues George's letters were usually very upbeat and refreshing. I looked forward to receiving them. George rarely had any negative comments about anyone. However in one letter he expressed concern for Leon Spinks and said he was worried "the parasites of boxing would get their hands on Leon."

George always remembered many of his old friends. In a letter from Phoenix, dated November 27, 1978, he talked about a former friend. "Hello Jerry: Received your very welcome letter, was happy to hear you and the rest of your family are all well. I am glad you are in contact with Sammy Luftspring. We boxed on amateur and pro programs together at least five times. He also has a very nice night club. I was there with him a few times. He is a real gentleman and friend, I think a lot of him. He always treated me great. I boxed with him when he was Canadian Champ, he was a great fighter. Also when he went to New York I used to meet him sometimes at the gym. Today he could easily be a world champion for he had class and could box real well and had a knockout punch in either hand." He went on to say "When you write him again give him my best wishes, also tell him to stay well. The weather here today was seventy degrees, and dry which helps me a lot. I hope the weather there is pleasant. So Jerry give my regards to all, and stay well and happy, George Pace."

George and I kept in touch and when he would be back in Cleveland we would speak on the phone weekly and sometimes get together at his place on the eastside of Cleveland. We also would go out to eat lunch together now and then.

George continued to be in and out of the VA Hospital and it never surprised me when he would call from his room there. Eventually his heart gave out and he died on July 20, 1984. He was only 69 years old. He was a good man and I cherish our years together.

Joey Maxim was a native Clevelander who did our city proud, becoming the World Light-heavyweight Champion in 1950. By the time I got seriously involved with boxing and began writing, Joey was no longer living in Cleveland. He spent many years in Florida and also Las Vegas, but he would come home now and then to visit his family, his brothers and his dear mother who lived to be 101. So eventually I would catch up with him when he was in Cleveland. We did correspond through letters.

Later on Joey and I were at different events together including boxing dinners such as the yearly ones held in Rochester, New York. We did keep in touch sporadically. I recall a conversation I had with the great Jim Jacobs regarding a request by Joey to obtain videos of some of his major fights. Jim Jacobs was a great guy but also very protective of his great film collection. He asked me to have Joey sign an affidavit stating he would only use the videos for personal entertainment. Joey did sign it and I was able to get him a very nice collection of many of his major battles including fights with Freddie Mills, Archie Moore, Irish Bob Murphy, Sugar Ray Robinson and Floyd Patterson.

From time to time I would send Joey photos to have him sign for friends and fellow fans. In a letter dated July 1985, Joey wrote, "Dear Jerry, I am glad to hear from you again & these pictures are really nice. I am going to sign one of them & keep the other. My wife likes it very much, if you have another one send it & I'll sign it and pay for the postage, okay?" He remarked "I wish you were coming to Las Vegas in October after Los Angeles. I might not get there, if you get here I am at the Frontier Hotel. I am dealing the big six wheel. Well so long & say hello to all there. Regards, Joey Maxim."

Sometime later my parents were on a trip to Las Vegas. I told them if they got a chance to go and see Joey Maxim at the Frontier Hotel. I don't remember where they were staying but it was a much longer walk than they had anticipated. When they got to the Frontier they asked where Joey was and sure enough he was working the wheel. He had never met my parents but they introduced themselves, and Joey smiled and was very friendly toward them especially after they told him they were from Cleveland and the parents of boxing historian Jerry Fitch. He signed some cards that had a photo of himself with the championship belt on and he spoke very highly of me. They told me Joey was very nice. I also remember my dad complaining about the supposed "dry heat" in Vegas. He said something very colorful about the dry heat, said his tongue was hanging out by the time they walked back to their hotel.

Archie Moore, the former Light-heavyweight Champion I met later in my boxing journey. Ironically we first corresponded before I ever met him in person. He had become a subscriber to a boxing newsletter I published at the time. It was called *Collector's Corner* and it came out monthly for about four years. This was before the days of computers and Ebay and the whole of my effort was to offer people a chance to buy and sell boxing memorabilia. For the price of the newsletter subscribers would get a free ad for a few issues. I also had a section where I would write boxing stories. Archie saw a story I wrote about the passing of former heavyweight contender Buddy Baer and thus wrote me. He usually did if he saw a story of interest. He more than likely never cared about boxing memorabilia, but he did like the stories and loved to comment on them.

I did eventually meet up with Archie in person out in Los Angeles and we continued to correspond for several years. I was always amazed at how sharp he was. He may have misspelled words at times but you could tell he was a very bright man with a keen wit and insight to a lot of things. One of the letters he sent me was written on August 11, 1986. It is quite lengthy but it is worth presenting it exactly as he typed it to me.

Dear Jerry, your Collector's Corner sheet hit my hand a few days ago. Greedily, I tore it open, and began to devour the dichomony [sic] therein presented. Your opening began with a Pitch from Fitch after which began the Snitch. The passage of Buddy on the long road perhaps to meet Max the older brother. Max was a terrific champion, colorful and playful, because he realized his awesome hitting power might severely injure an opponent, after Frankie Campbell's death from Maxie's blows, the fire that lighted Maxie's candle of intent was doused with sorrow, and the colorful career was over. Max refereed as did Mushy Callahan, and Harry Kessler some bouts I was in. I can't feel any anger for Harry Kessler anymore, all Kessler lost was my complete respect, with his unexplained aribitration[sic] in the 12/17/52 bout with Joey Maxim in St. Louis, with me taking 13 of the 15 rds. Kessler's score was fairly close.

Archie went on to say,

Moore vs. Rocky...Again fate decreed Kessler should referee this match a dream come true, a dream complex with innunendos [sic] and much publicity abashing Rocky Marciano for his refusal to meet the true contender, if he (Rocky) claimed to be champion. Kessler did not use his goading tactics nor did he have to...Rd. 1 I met Rocky in ring center, and the Rock backed off circling around as if he was "casing" me. Not without the reciepton [sic] of a few stiff left jabs I felt that if he continued to look me over he'd surely get ko'd. Having felt sure that the first round was mine, unsurprisingly Marciano came swinging furiously. The Rock missed several overhand shots, then here comes the bomb, a looping overhand right, I pull back for the counter, but my right foot slips as my right uppercut dents Rock's chin. Falling forward, but saving himself from falling on his face by landing with both elbows and right knee. Ah' gotcha now, and you won't get away. Rocky is up at two, back turned to me gazing out with both elbows resting on the top strand of the ring rope, as if appealing to the crowd for being upstaged by the mouthy Light-heavy champ. Excitedly Kessler wiped my gloves (stalling for time) meanwhile my corner is screaming hysterically, "hit im, hit im, there aint no 8 count, hit im." I'm trying to sight Marciano in, but Kessler orders me to a neutral corner. The fight fans are wild and the noise is deafening, now Kessler has lost the count and starts at four, shoving me away from Marciano with his butt. Then as if no one was watching Kessler gave Rocky a quick hard jerk as he released Marciano's gloves. All this action was deleted from the film as they went to the theatres for public consumption. And the film will never be found, at least while I am around. It was too bad that critics refuse to acknowledge that Rocky needed the help that Kessler supplied him that September night in 1955. I held no grudge nor anamosity [sic] toward Rocky, nor any of the men I fought during my ring career.

There was more to this letter but you get the gist of what his letters were like. I have managed to save a few of them. Archie's letters were never dull and I always looked forward to seeing them arrive in my mailbox. He really sent me some doozy letters, I never knew what to expect. He was not afraid to tell it like it was. Archie liked to use big words, he certainly didn't write like any fighter I had ever met at that time. You would never know he had been a boxer all those years and participated in 186 fights, probably more.

Lloyd Marshall and I never exchanged a single letter in the years we knew each other. Any correspondence I had with him went through his wife Mazie. I didn't even talk to Lloyd on the phone until perhaps 1980. Naturally I knew all about him, his reputation in the Cleveland boxing circles was legendary. When people talked about the many Cleveland boxing greats the names Johnny Kilbane, Johnny Risko, Jimmy Bivins and Joey Maxim always were part of the conversation. Lloyd Marshall was also added to that list of Cleveland greats.

I read everything I could about Lloyd before I ever wrote a single word about him. In those days besides the Ring Record Books I often went to the Cleveland Public Library downtown and spent hours scanning through microfilm. It was a joy to find the old sports pages of the various Cleveland newspapers and read about the many great fights that were held in Cleveland over the years. I learned a lot about Lloyd Marshall during those trips to the library.

Needless to say some of the best information I ever learned about Lloyd came from former fighters who still lived in Cleveland at the time and either grew up with Lloyd or spent time in various local gyms with him. I do not recall who eventually gave me an address for Lloyd Marshall, who had lived in California since the late 1930s. Regardless I typed up a letter and sent it to the address given to me in Sacramento, California. Before too much time went by my phone rang and the lady on the other end identified herself as Mazie Marshall, Lloyd's wife.

I will never forget that first conversation with Lloyd Marshall when Mazie handed him the phone. It would be the first of many. But the thing I remember most is how we kept in touch often and for whatever reason Mazie could not get it in her head to remember the time difference between California and Ohio. More than a few times she called me at a ridiculous hour of night and usually woke me up from a dead sleep. You would have thought after a while I would turn off my phone but the fact was my job often consisted of phone calls at crazy hours asking me to come into work to fill the void of someone who had called off. So I always wanted to have the phone on. I tried to be polite and I did tell Mazie more than once about the current time in Ohio when she called. She would apologize but then a week or so later the same thing would happen. It always surprised me how often Mazie would call because this was before the days of cell phones and long distance calling was rather expensive.

At the time Lloyd Marshall's mother still lived on the eastside of Cleveland. He had not seen her in years, probably since the 1940s when he came back to Cleveland for a series of fights for promoter Larry Atkins. During our phone conversations he would casually mention that he wanted to come home to see his elderly mother and visit with old boxing friends.

I often mentioned it to Mazie that it sure would be great if they could come back to Cleveland to visit. Mazie was not from Cleveland but had been here a few times sitting ringside, including the night Lloyd completely destroyed Ezzard Charles in eight rounds in 1943. She often was called "Ringside Mazie." She said she was Lloyd's good luck charm and the only reason Lloyd lost to Jimmy Bivins was because she had not made the trip.

Much to my surprise in July of 1983 I received a call informing me that Lloyd was coming back to Cleveland for a visit. I was excited to say the least that I was going to meet the amazing Lloyd Marshall. Mazie then told me that she would not be coming to Cleveland with Lloyd and that he was taking the trip on a Greyhound bus. I almost fell off my seat. I could not imagine being on a bus for that long. I didn't question her, just asked what day and time was he due to arrive.

Best laid plans don't always work out. On the morning Lloyd was due into Cleveland I met Jimmy Bivins down at the bus terminal. Jimmy wanted to surprise Lloyd. Well, the bus was late and when it arrived there was no Lloyd Marshall on it! I had to go to work so Jimmy said he would check during the day and see if Lloyd was on a later bus. In the afternoon after coming home from work Jimmy Bivins phoned me and said Lloyd had arrived and that he had taken him over to his mother's house.

Lloyd's trip to Cleveland lasted a week or so. Jimmy Bivins, George Pace and another former fighter named Chuck Watkins escorted Lloyd around town, took him to gyms and to visit former friends and fighters. They kept him on the go. Chuck Watkins wore a hearing aid and said it was his claim to fame. Of course I asked him why? He said because in a sparring session with Lloyd Marshall his eardrum had been ruptured and his ear was never right after that. He felt it was a badge of honor.

I personally set up an interview with then Sports Editor, Hal Lebovitz at the Plain Dealer. We all had a nice time and Hal wrote a nice story about Lloyd and Jimmy that appeared in the Plain Dealer on July 19, 1983.

Another fond memory was when Jimmy Bivins and George Pace brought Lloyd out to our Parma Boxing Club. We had a fun time and a couple other former Golden Glove fighters from back in Lloyd's day showed up. A lot of great photos were taken by my friend Terry Gallagher, including one showing Lloyd and Jimmy doing a reenactment of their classic battle of June 8, 1943 in Cleveland Municipal Stadium before 18,000 rain soaked fans. That was a defense of Jimmy Bivins' "Duration" Light-heavyweight title which Jimmy won with a 13th round knockout. Lloyd and Jimmy posed with Lloyd choking Jimmy with the ring ropes, 43 years after their fight. That photo has appeared in two of my previous books.

After Lloyd went back to California I eventually was able to send him some nice photos from his Cleveland visit. Mazie called and thanked me and told me that they loved the photos.

As the years went by the phone calls became fewer and fewer. Eventually I heard Mazie had passed and by then I had lost all contact with the family. On August 4, 1997 Lloyd joined Mazie.

Ezzard Charles was a great fighter and unfortunately I was only able to meet him once. I never had a correspondence with him. Our brief encounter at the Cleveland Arena in 1964 consisted of me asking him if he was Ezzard Charles, watching him say yes and go into a shadow boxing routine as I stood in awe. I got his autograph and never saw him again. I did eventually have a different kind of correspondence involving Ezzard Charles.

Sadly Ezzard suffered for many years with ALS (Amyotrophic lateral sclerosis) also known as Lou Gehrig's disease. He died from it on May 28, 1975 at the age of 53. It was a sad ending for the man called "The Cincinnati Cobra," who even now is being called one of the greatest pound for pound fighters ever. Some people speculate that Ezzard may have already been suffering from ALS near the end of his career but I have never seen any proof of that.

I was involved with the now defunct The World Boxing Hall of Fame in Los Angeles for a number of years. I was actually one of the original members of The Board of Directors. Years later I was contacted by one of the officers and asked to track down Ezzard Charles' family. The group inducted Ezzard Charles posthumously in their Hall of Fame in 1983.

Anyway The World Boxing Hall of Fame never located anyone in Charles' family to give his Hall of Fame plaque to. For whatever reason they felt I was the man for the job of locating a family member. I remember reading that Ezzard Charles had lived in Chicago after his ring days so that is where I decided to first look.

Once again this was before computers and so I tried other methods. Eventually one of my contacts in Chicago sent me an address that he felt might be the right one. So I sent off a letter in May of 1989 and hoped for the best. Sometime shortly after May 12, 1989 I received a letter from Mrs. Gladys Charles. She stated she was the widow of Ezzard Charles.

Back then as now I came across con artists who claimed they were a former fighter or someone famous. There were stories about these phonies all the time. I had personally encountered a fake Jimmy Bivins, eventually heard about a fake Johnny Risko and a man impersonating Tony Zale. So I wanted to be sure I had the correct family.

When I think back now I feel bad because I told Gladys Charles that before I would mail off the plaque I needed proof I had the right person, the right family. I know it must have been an imposition for her but I wanted the plaque to end up in the correct hands, especially after so much time had passed since The World Boxing Hall of Fame had actually inducted Ezzard.

Gladys Charles sent me more than enough documentation. Among the list of items she sent me were a copy of statements by Ezzard and her applying for their Marriage License, a copy of the Real Estate Contract for their house in Chicago and the Death Certificate for Ezzard, plus a photocopy of her Drivers License, all notarized.

I mailed off the plaque and received a very nice thank you letter to acknowledge that she had received it. The letter was dated June 8, 1989.

In my collection of letters and postcards I also have letters from Anton Christoforidis, Gene Fullmer, Joey Giardello, Danny "Little Red" Lopez, Lou Nova, Earnie Shavers, Kid Gavilan, Bobby "Schoolboy" Chacon, Doyle Baird and Larry Holmes. Back then I also communicated with many others such as Sammy Angott, George Nichols and Jimmy Mclarnin to name just a few. In the case of Jimmy McLarnin, other than exchanging Christmas cards we always talked on the telephone. His greeting was always the same, "Hello Champ".

Frankie Garcia is another former fighter I met while visiting Southern California during 1975-85. He was at the time a good friend of my very special friend, George Luckman. He also was President of the Golden State Boxers Association. When we met he still lived in a suburb of Los Angeles. Later he and his wife moved to Sun City, California, a retirement community. George Luckman and I visited there a few times. Frankie was a great guy and quite a character too.

Frankie Garcia had been a professional boxer as a featherweight in the 1920s and participated in over 90 bouts. He met some excellent fighters in his career including Sammy Mandell, Freddy Dawson, Johnny Dundee and Kid Williams.

He and I wrote letters back and forth for a number of years. For some reason one dated March 18, 1978, I kept out of all of them. As usual I will type this just as Frankie did back then. Sun City, California, March 18, 1978.

> Mi querido cuate Jerry, Comoestas amigo? I just went for a walk around the City and back home....feeling just great...been in the Sun for a couple days now and if I am not too careful I will be taken for a Mexican.....Wow the sun out

here is really burning, every day its NINETY and feels like a hundred and two...Bub Thomas writes me and will be out here to visit in May.....He is now in Orlando, Florida....He will get a real surprise when he sees all his cartoons and pictures on our wall.....YOU look great too! ...

Jerry we sure will be glad to see you and "Punchy" is already on the look out for you.....people stop and take pictures of Punchy all the time and he doesn't mind...the more we live here the more we love it...we are on the go all the time...Elsie just brought me a WESTERN shirt with beautiful buttons and embroidery that's made to order for me...makes me look like Pancho Villa!...bought it at a garage sale for two and a half....must be worth at least forty bucks....Jerry wait till you see all the stuff she bought for the house at garage sales...bought a cabinet file case for forty dollars and its worth at least three hundred...now we are set to file and put away all our junk and what not. ...

Stay well pal and thanks for the photos and letter. ... Please write again and soon. My beautiful broad sends her love too. Adios and good luck, Frankie Garcia.

NOTE: Punchy was a lawn statue that was a sort of caricature of a battered fighter that sat in his front yard for everyone to see.

Sometimes I miss those simpler times when people actually sat down and composed a letter.

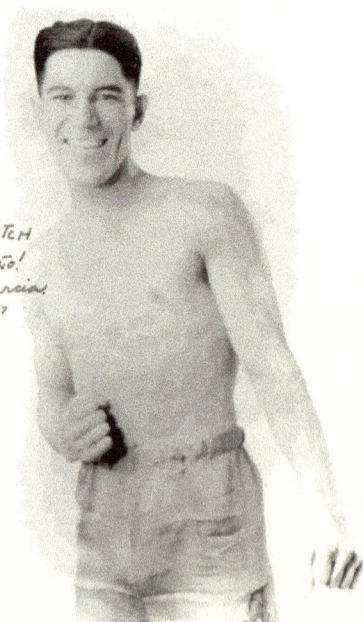

To JERRY FITCH
SALUD AMIGO!
Frankie Garcia
1/31/77

The First Interview At King's Gym

By John J. Raspanti

The first time I heard of Andre Ward was when he boxed in the 2004 Olympic Games. He wasn't considered a favorite. He was good, but how good was the big question.

Then he won the gold. The pundits reactions didn't come close to earlier times when they celebrated America's Olympians. Ward turned pro a few months after the Olympics in 2004. He won by stoppage in two. After weeks of nagging his promotional company for an interview, I sat down to talk with him after he had won 21 fights in a row.

There was a little buzz around him, but the ink was more about when he was wobbled in one of his earlier fights, or knocked down by Darnell Boone in 2007. I had been ringside when Ward, 25, faced his toughest test against former title challenger, Edson Miranda. The hard-hitting Columbian had predicted he'd knock out Ward, implying that Ward had a weak chin. He cracked Ward with some hard shots, but didn't come close to beating him. Ward trained at a place called King's Gym in Oakland.

The gym is dark and dusky, and groans with age and gravitas. There are boxing posters and pictures of fighters on the walls. Many are old and worn, like the gentleman I nodded to sitting on a bench near the ring. Ward would be fighting WBA super middleweight champion, Mikkel Kessler, in nine days, making him the underdog again. I quickly realized that Ward thrives on being underestimated. I ask the old guy if he's seen Ward. He points towards the back part of the ring. I spot Ward sitting slightly behind a ring post. He's alone and staring at something only he can see. As I approach and nod, he smiles. We shake hands and go find a place to sit down and talk. It's an old bench a few feet from the ring. Loud music blasts from the speakers above us. As our eyes meet, I can sense the edge he has, that hunger and the drive that it takes to win a world championship. Fight day is nearing. I ask him how he tapers down his training. "Physically," says Ward, "we have our days where we back up…but mentally, it's going to be a mental grind when it's over. Everyday it's the (fight) on on your mind. That doesn't stop until the fight is over."

Ward liked football and loved baseball while growing up in Hayward, CA. His father, Frank, instilled in him his love for boxing. "My dad raised me along with my brother," Ward said. "He would tell me stories of when he boxed. He was fifteen and zero as an amateur. He kept telling me stories of his rivals and how he prepared. That was enough for me. I told my dad I wanted to do it, I wanted to give it (boxing) a shot. He told me OK, but I'd have to stick with it. That's the kind of father he was. You do something you're going to give it all you have. That was his mindset."

Though I had researched Ward's background before our interview, I wasn't aware that his father had died in 2002. I was surprised when he told me. I immediately flashed on the Olympic Games, and asked Ward how difficult it must have been to win the gold, and not have his dad with him to celebrate. "Unbelievable," Ward said. "The bitter sweetness of it. I was like, Wow! I'm happy, I'm excited with the accomplishment of winning, and to this day, it still feels surreal. Nobody can take that from you. But as you just mentioned my father wasn't there. So. That's what put a damper on things. But that's life."

Ward grew up admiring Roy Jones Jr. He appreciated the way Jones took care of his business inside the ring. But even more, how Jones was his own man out of it. Ward was striving to be the same kind of guy as Jones in and out of the ring. He would achieve his goals.

When I told my late father that I was going to interview Ward, he was curious if Ward would support his own sons if they expressed interest in boxing. "I would but I'm going to really discourage it," said Ward. "This is a tough business and it's especially tough when you're coming behind your father. They know this is what dad is doing for this season of his life, but it doesn't necessarily mean you have to jump into it. So I'm going to discourage it." Ward's nickname was S.O.G (son of God) when he boxed. Some didn't like it. Ward didn't care. "My father ingrained that in me," Ward said. "My personal relationship with Jesus Christ, that's everything to me."

Earlier I mentioned the seeming lack of hoopla when Ward won the gold. I had to ask him about it. He looked away before answering me. "You know it's a tough question because I'm not somebody who looks for that," he said. "It's tough to ask me that. It's a very logical question but, I don't really give it much thought. I'm aware that I didn't get a lot of attention like the seventy-six and eighty-four team got. Or even the money. There're some good reasons for that. They went right on TV and fought on *The Wide World of Sports*. We fought at two or three in the morning on a network that nobody knew about. But I don't want to make it seem like I got short-changed. I do see the disparity. Yeah."

Ward told me he's unbelievably competitive. Doesn't like to lose in anything. I'm pretty competitive myself, but I could feel Ward's edgy desire. I saw this first hand a few years later at King's Gym. Ward was in training for his fight with Arthur Abraham. Trainer Virgil Hunter had hired three fighters to emulate Abraham's style. The first boxer seemed to be in a bad mood. As they prepared to spar, the other boxer started disparaging Ward. I looked up from what I was doing to watch. First he called Ward names, then he said he wasn't "fucking impressed." Ward stared at him and said nothing. The bell rang. Ward worked on his defense and clipped the guy with jabs. His mouth was still working. Major trash talk. It was obvious Ward was getting annoyed. He started to talk back. The bell rang. Ward went back to his corner. I noticed that the other fighter's mouth was bleeding. Ward pointed at him, and, after the bell rang, met him in the middle of the ring. The beatdown commenced immediately. Ward landed shots down the middle. Crimson dripped from the other boxer's nose. And mouth. Hunter stopped the action after two minutes. The other fighter staggered to his corner. I heard Ward say, "I warned you." I guess. A few minutes later, the boxer walked to Ward's corner. He put his hand out and said something. Ward took it and nodded. He didn't smile.

Throughout his career, Ward's style drew comments. Some would say he fought like former world champion, Bernard Hopkins. I asked him to describe it. "Formless," he said with a smile. "I don't really have a style. Kessler you can describe his style. The closest they come with me is, he's a boxer. But I don't really think that's accurate because I don't really get the credit for my physicality, my toughness." Ward told me his toughest fight at that point had been against Miranda. He ate some solid right hands. He told me that you "condition yourself to minimize the punches." Fighters are a different breed. Pain is not supposed to bother them. I eyed one of the banners on the wall at the gym: *"Real boxers are ordinary people with extra-ordinary determination."* And another: *"The harder you train the luckier you get."*

I didn't see much luck that day when I spoke with Ward. He was a man on a mission. The so-called experts were wrong the night he fought Kessler. Twenty-eight of thirty-one picked Kessler to win. I had picked Ward. I was leaning towards Ward even before our interview. Talking to him cemented it. I was ringside for the bout. Ward cleaned Kessler's clock. He was awkward and physical. Some, including Kessler, said he was dirty. Sour grapes. Kessler looked confused and thoroughly beaten. Ward stood near his corner waiting to hear "And the new super middleweight champion." He raised his hand and pointed to the sky. I flashed back to our interview. His dream was to be a champion.

REAL BOXERS ARE ORDINARY PEOPLE WITH EXTRA-ORDINARY DETERMINATION

Over the next few years, I'd be ringside for number of his fights. Ward was never a pretty fighter like Sugar Ray Robinson and Muhammad Ali. He's a talented boxer, but his grit is his greatest strength. I noticed that grit that first time I interviewed him. It was in his eyes. Nobody would deny him. Ward strived for greatness, and in my view, achieved it.

He never lost a professional fight.

Often Forgotten Middleweight Contenders From The 1950s

By Jerry Fitch

One of my favorite weight divisions outside of the heavyweights has always been the middleweights. During the 1950s there were so many excellent fighters that it is hard to remember all of them.

Avid historians or people who followed boxing during that time frame may know some of the fighters I write about in this chapter. I am pretty sure a lot of younger fans and even some of us oldtimers might tend to forget just how many very good men were in the middleweight division during the 1950s. I will have to admit that although I do remember some of the fighters I write about in this chapter, I hardly remember who they fought and how they were ranked during this special time in boxing history.

I think it is safe to assume most true fight fans are familiar with the names Joey Giardello, Bobo Olson, Rocky Castellani, Randy Turpin, Joey Giambra, Carmen Basilio, Gene Fullmer, Bobby Dykes, Ralph "Tiger" Jones, Paul Pender and Henry Hank. Of course anyone who doesn't remember Sugar Ray Robinson, what can I say.

I went through *The Ring* magazine ratings from the 1950s and picked out a dozen of the many forgotten contenders from that time. Although many may not be as well-known as the men I listed above, they were however very good fighters, competitive and worthy of their status in the middleweight division during their careers. All of the men I write about in this chapter were in the top ten rankings during the 1950s.

Bobby Boyd was born on October 25, 1933 in Chicago, Illinois. As a pro he was active during the years 1952-1961, engaging in 71 professional fights and had a record of 54-14-3. He fought most of the big names during his time and had wins over Holly Mims, Willie Vaughn, Rocky Castellani and Gene Fullmer. He also met Spider Webb, Rory Calhoun, George Benton and lost by a kayo to Joey Giardello. He hit the top ten during 1957-58. He was a competitive fighter. He was only 68 when he died on June 21, 2002.

Rory Calhoun was born Herman Calhoun in Georgia on September 29, 1935. The name he fought under was the same as a Hollywood actor. I remember when I met him in 1985. I heard the name Rory Calhoun and because we were in Hollywood, I wasn't sure which Calhoun he was until I walked up to him and introduced myself. I have to admit at the time I was hoping it was the fighter not the actor. He was active from 1954-1962 and finished his career with a record of 45-15-2. I remember Rory Calhoun the fighter because I did see some of the Friday Night Fights, where he appeared 27 times.

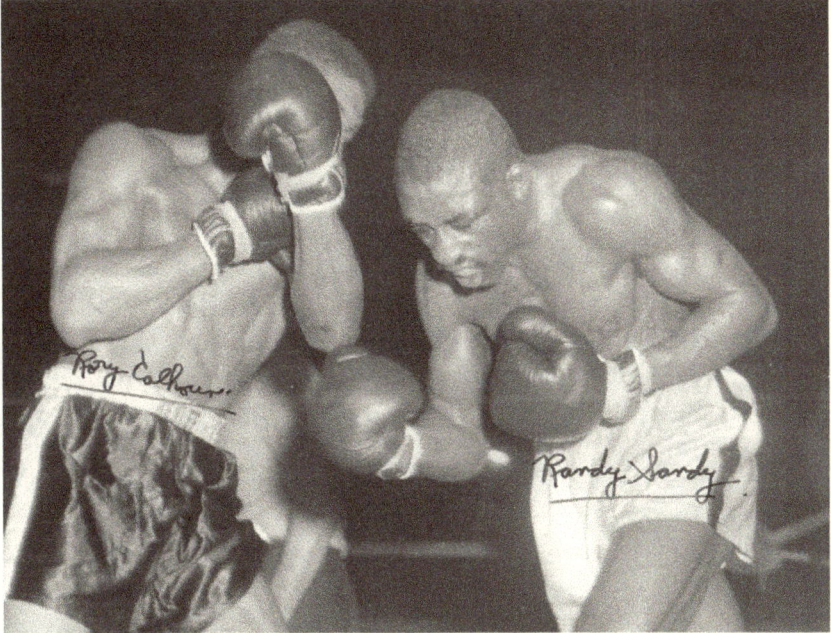

Rory had wins over Randy Sandy, Willie Vaughn, Charley Cotton, Dick Tiger, Ralph Tiger Jones, Rocky Castellani, Joey Giambra and Bobby Boyd. Many of his losses were to excellent fighters such as Spider Webb, Bobo Olson, Henry Hank, Joey Giambra, Florentino Fernandez, Joey Giardello and Jimmy Ellis. His name appeared in the middleweight top ten from 1956-1958 and later in 1961. He died on February 15, 1988, of liver failure. He was only 53 years old.

Ernie Durando was born Armando Ernest Durando in Bayonne, New Jersey on April 7, 1926. He was known as "The Rock" during his career because he had a devastating right hand. He was another contender who was not an easy nut to crack and he appeared in the middleweight top ten in 1951 and 1952. His career record was 46-23-4, scoring 31 knockouts.

Ernie held career wins over Steve Belloise, Joey DeJohn, Paddy Young, Rocky Castellani, Charles Humez, and Bobby Dykes. His losses were often to very good fighters such as Jimmy Flood, Harold Green (twice), Rocky Castellani (twice), Paddy Young (twice), Ralph "Tiger" Jones, Paul Pender, Joey Giardello (twice), and Gene Fullmer. Ernie passed in May of 1992 at the age of 66.

Eugene Hairston was known as "Silent Hairston" because he was deaf. He became the first deaf fighter to become really well known during his career. There were a few other deaf fighters throughout boxing history however Hairston became more well known because he was fighting in many large cities and arenas against big name opponents. A red light was put in the corner of the rings he fought in to signal to him that the round was ending.

Hairston was a native of Harlem, New York, born there in 1929. His career was rather short but he managed to pack in 63 bouts during that time. He fought from 1947-1952 and had a final record of 45-13-5.

Eugene hit the top ten as early as 1950. His wins came against the likes of Charley Williams, Lee Sala, Artie Towne, Paul Pender and Laurent Dauthuille. I recall he also held two victories over Cleveland's Jackie Keough. His losses were mostly to other contenders and champions such as Bobo Olson, Jake LaMotta, Kid Gavilan and Johnny Bratton. He also met Charles Humez, Walter Cartier and Rocky Castellani. He lived to be 85 years old and died on December 3, 2012.

Charles Humez was a French fighter who fought from 1948 to 1958. He had an outstanding record of 94-7-1 with 47 kayo wins. The vast majority of his early fights were in Europe so it is hard to tell much about his opponents and fights held during that time. *The Ring* magazine, which posted the ratings during his time, apparently thought very highly of him. He was listed in the top ten middleweights in 1952 and 1954-1957. His best wins were against Pierre Langlois, Jean Walzack, Laurent Dauthuille, Tony Janiro, Gene Hairston, Gustav Sholz, Ralph "Tiger" Jones and Peter Muller.

Charles Humez losses were to very good fighters including Gene Fullmer, Randy Turpin, Ernie Durando, Gustav Sholz and Ralph "Tiger" Jones. Charles Humez died in France in 1979. He was only 52 years old.

Charley Joseph was a New Orleans fighter that I truly do not remember. Upon close examination I found out he was a very capable fighter. Born in 1933, he turned pro in 1951 and campaigned until 1961. His record of 52-13-1 included victories over Holly Mims, Charley Cotton, Willie Vaughn, Spider Webb, Randy Sandy, George Benton and Henry Hank. His losses included

Freddie Little, Henry Hank, George Benton, Bobby Boyd and Spider Webb.

I found his name listed in the top ten in 1956 & 1957. He may not be as recognizable as many of the other contenders I am writing about because he rarely ventured away from his native New Orleans and Louisiana in general. However it is obvious he was a force to be reckoned with. He passed on July 14, 2005 at age 72.

Holly Mims is a name that pops up from time to time because he is often thought of as one of the most hard luck fighters ever. He was born on February 10, 1929 in Washington D.C. and campaigned as a professional from 1948-1967. His record of 68-28-6 is nothing to sneeze at. However he is also well known because he always seemed to be on the short end of decision losses, in important fights. This stymied him throughout his career. He had more than a dozen split decision losses in his career and several majority decision losses that could also have gone either way.

Mims would fight anyone, anytime and because of that he wasn't always given a fair shake. His loss to Ruben Carter in 1962 was taken on one day's notice. He flew into New York City just prior to the fight and even dropped Carter in the 4th round. Mims had very fast hands and was an excellent boxer. He did not have great power and only scored 13 knockouts during his career.

Holly Mims was very good and always highly regarded, proof of which was reflected in the middleweight ratings where he appeared in the top ten often in 1953-1955 and 1958-1959, even a few times in other years.

When I was in my teens there was a place called Jean's Funny House, aka Jean's Fun House in downtown Cleveland. In that store there were all sorts of old fashioned arcade games and novelties and you could also buy Exhibit Boxing Cards from a machine. I don't remember the exact cost at the time but the first card that came out for me was Holly Mims. The second one was Cuban boxer Isaac Logart and the third was Floyd Patterson.

Sadly Holly Mims died of a kidney ailment in his beloved Washington D.C. on January 13, 1970. He was only 42 years old.

Lee Sala is a name I must admit I was not very familiar with at all. That is the beauty of checking the old articles, records and ratings from the 1950s. You learn a lot. Lee was born in Donora, Pa. in 1926. He was active as a professional from 1946-1953. He engaged in 83 fights with a record of 76-7 with 48 knockout wins. Quite impressive in my mind. I found him ranked as high as #6 in the top ten in 1952. I suspect he appeared in the top ten other times.

Some of Lee's major wins were against the likes of Reuben Jones, Jackie Armitage, Joey DeJohn, Sammy Secreet, Jackie Burke and Joe Rindone. Lee had losses to good opponents including Willie Troy, Bobo Olson, Billy Kilgore and Eugene Hairston. He lived to be 85 years old, dying on December 3, 2012.

Willie Troy is a fighter I do remember but only because I read about his fights with Joey Giardello and Floyd Patterson and actually have watched footage from those two contests. Willie was born on September 6, 1932, in Norfolk, Virginia. One of the things that stood out was that Willie was tough and could take punishment without going down. In the Giardello and Patterson fights he took such a pounding that the ring doctor visited Troy's corner in both fights and advised the referee to halt the fight because he had taken too much punishment.

Willie had a rather short career from 1951-1956, engaging in 41 fights and finishing with a 33-6-2 slate, scoring 23 knockouts. He met most of the best fighters in the division in this short span, scoring victories over Bobby Dykes, Del Flanagan, Walter Cartier, Tony Anthony and Randy Sandy. He was rated in the top ten in 1953 & 1954. His losses were to Clarence Hinnant, Joey Giardello, Floyd Patterson and in his last fight, Johnny Sullivan. He suffered a broken jaw against Sullivan and never fought again.

Artie Towne was born James Tufts on December 22, 1926 in New York. His professional career ran from 1944 to 1959. He fought often and finished with a career record of 94-16-1 scoring 43 knockouts. He was managed by Ross Harvey and George Gainford.

In addition to fighting in most major venues in the United States, Artie also had matches in Jamaica, Cuba, Peru, England, Germany and Canada. He held victories over Henry Brimm, Johnny Sullivan, Milo Savage, Yvon Durelle and Bert Lytell.

His name appeared in the top ten as late as 1955. His losses were to mostly good fighters such as Joe Blackwood, Eugene Hairston, Mauro Mina, Henry Brimm and Sam Baroudi.

Tragically he died in Harlem, New York on July 2, 1967, having been stabbed to death during a robbery attempt. He was only 40.

Willie Vaughn was born December 4, 1932, in Chandler, Texas. He fought as a professional from 1951-1959, with a career record of 45-22-11. His name appears as late as 1957 in the top ten Ring ratings.

Willie's career had many ups and downs but he did score some major wins against the likes of Earl Turner, Ralph Tiger Jones, Charley Joseph, Jimmy Beecham and he held Milo Savage to a draw. His losses were to very good fighters such as Joseph, Rory Calhoun, Bobo Olson, Spider Webb and Henry Hank. He also had a no-decision fight with Joey Giardello on March 25, 1957. Originally the fight was scored as a split decision win for Vaughn. The fight was supposed to be scored on the 5-point must system. However referee Ray Sissom inadvertently used the 10-point scoring system. The Missouri Athletic Commission later declared his card invalid and ordered the contest recorded as no-decision.

Willie fought mostly out of California in his early career, later on fought in many cities such as New York, New Orleans and Miami. He even fought in Australia and New Zealand. There is some nice video footage available of his loss on points to fellow American Jimmy Martinez on February 23, 1959 at Sydney Stadium in Australia.

Spider Webb was born Ellsworth Webb on November 11, 1931, in Tulsa, Oklahoma, but spent his formative years in Chicago, Illinois. He turned pro in 1953 and retired from boxing in 1961. His career record was 34-6-0, certainly not a lot of fights for an eight year period. However he packed a lot of great fights into his resume in that short period of time.

When all was said and done, Spider, considered a boxer-puncher, had done remarkably well in defeating Bobby Boyd, Rory Calhoun, Terry Downes, Willie Vaughn, Charley Joseph, Charley Cotton, Dick Tiger (In London, England) and Joey Giardello (a TKO on cuts). Because of those victories Spider found himself rated in the top ten of the division from 1956-1959.

Four of Webb's six losses were to major fighters in the middleweight division. He lost to champions Gene Fullmer (twice) and Dick Tiger, also perennial contenders Holly Mims and Charley Joseph.

The second time Spider Webb met Gene Fullmer on December 4, 1959 was in quest of Fullmer's NBA Middleweight Title. Gene had won that portion of the middleweight title over Carmen Basilio the previous August, in San Francisco via a 14th round TKO stoppage. Spider gave his all against Gene Fullmer in their Logan, Utah title fight but lost a 15-round unanimous decision.

Spider Webb passed on January 23, 2017 at the age of 86.

Five Favorite Fighters

By John J. Raspanti

The best way to compile this list is to go back to the beginning.

Muhammad Ali: My first memory of a living fighter wasn't because of his fistic abilities. No, it was quite simply his mouth. He was Cassius Clay then. A year later he was Muhammad Ali. He spouted poetry. Not even Moe, Larry, Curly, or even Superman could do that. I sensed he was controversial, but there was something likeable about him. He beat the "Big Ugly Bear" to win the heavyweight championship of the world. Ten years later, he regained it by stopping "The Mummy."

There were lots of fights in between. The Vietnam war was raging and Ali's "I aint got no quarrel with them Vietcong" lost his boxing license when his local draft board rejected his application as a conscientious objector.

When he returned in 1970, I was thrilled. Boxing wasn't the same without him. I sat by our stereo listening to the results of his comeback fights. His bout with "Smokin" Joe Frazier, aptly referred to as "The Fight" or "The Fight of the Century" on March 8, 1971, stopped the sporting world. Boxing was so popular back then, and Ali, through his antics, drew even more attention to it. There was no internet but Ali didn't need one. He was part promoter, part boxer. He ruffled feathers, and prepared for Frazier.

The fight was a war between two highly skilled and competitive athletes. Frazier won. I actually hated him for a while, but that soon changed to respect and admiration. Frazier was special, like Ali. We fans didn't realize it then because we took it for granted. Most boxers' careers are short. They have only so many fights in them. Damage is inflicted. Reflexes dull. Ali was a different fighter when he came back. Losing a half a step was all it took. When once he was able to lean back to avoid a blow, now, more often than not, they landed. Ali was blessed with a great chin. He could absorb and fight back. He defeated the invincible George Foreman in 1974 with guile and guts. I watched Foreman train a few months before. His powerful punches put a dent in the heavy bag. *The Ring* magazine told me that he would do the same to the 32-year-old Ali. Instead, Ali regained the heavyweight championship with a stunning 8th round knockout. He said he was retiring, but nobody believed him.

In the 1970s, I was able to see a number of Ali's fights on TV or tape delay. He went to hell and back one more time with Frazier. Their third match was beautiful brutality. Ali had nothing to prove, but kept fighting. Everything about him was slower, including his speech. His victory over Earnie Shavers was like teetering on a roof top. When Leon Spinks took Ali's crown a year later, I felt sick. I was elated when he came back and defeated Spinks in a rematch. He finally retired, but came back one more time. What a waste. All for money. He was in his 40s when Parkinson's disease attacked him. He fought back the best he could, but was eventually rendered speechless.

Ali often called himself "The Greatest." Many agree. To me, even with his obvious gifts, he was much more than just a fighter. He was a man of great courage and fortitude, in and out of the ring.

Mando Ramos: I first learned of Ramos from my grandfather and *The Ring* magazine.

Grandpa would rave about Ramos and chuckle, like he knew more than the pundits.

He probably did. Ramos was a boxing prodigy. A natural with worn gloves. He could box or slug. He preferred slugging. In Los Angeles, he was a matinee idol, loved by women and idolized by men. His smile lit up the room. He was the youngest lightweight world champion in history, and completely shot at 24. I didn't know what that meant when I was following his career, but his fall stunned me. He was like a shooting star who appears from nowhere, wows and amazes, and then, in the blink of an eye, is gone. Many of his fights were brutal. Ramos had a huge heart, but little discipline. Former champion, Carlos Palomino, told me years later that Ramos, who rarely slept, said he'd "rest while his opponent threw punches."

I remember his grudge fight with former sparring partner Raul Rojas in 1970. Rojas told reporters a few weeks before the fight that he expected to win by knockout. A knockout did occur, only, it was Rojas who found himself on his back in round six. His career was short but brilliant. He regained the title but lost it soon after. Ramos was done. Drugs and alcohol had done the deed. But his star would last. Boxing fans never forgot. For a short time, Mando Ramos was the most popular human in Los Angeles. He was Oscar De La Hoya before the golden one was born.

Armando Muniz: He wasn't a natural like Mando Ramos. Or fleet of foot like Muhammad Ali. He had had short arms and was usually at a disadvantage. Nothing he did wowed anyone, but he was plucky, gutsy, nervy, could punch, and was tough. Real tough. It's no coincidence that Muniz was nicknamed, "The Man." I first saw him one late Saturday night on TV, of course. It was at the Olympic Auditorium in Los Angeles where he fought an amazing 23 times. He was fighting slick Bobby Watts. Muniz was five inches shorter and half a step behind. No matter, he pounded on Watts, soon to be called "Boogaloo," and won by decision. Watts was disconsolate after the fight. Muniz went to his corner and talked to him. I liked that. Respectful and gracious. Muniz fought at the Olympic every few weeks. His brawl with Oscar Albarado brought down the house.

Then he fought former welterweight and middleweight champion, Emile Griffith. Muniz entered the ring undefeated. He exited a first-time loser. I watched it a week after the bout went down. Griffith was cute, tricky, and talented. Muniz kept trying, but it wasn't nearly enough. After a squabble over money with Olympic promoter, Aileen Eaton, Muniz hit the road. He captured the NABF welterweight crown by knocking out Percy Pugh in two. After splitting his next two fights, he stopped talented Adolph Pruitt in eight rounds at the Convention Center in Anaheim, CA. Years after the fight, Muniz told me his victory over Pruitt was one of his greatest ring achievements. Pruitt had fought for a world title and was ranked above Muniz. The fighters went toe-to-toe until a combination floored Pruitt. Pruitt beat the count, but the referee waved the fight off.

Muniz lost his title to Eddie Perkins, but bounced back to starch upset-minded Billy Lloyd. A win over talented Hedgemon Lewis set up a dream welterweight title shot against champion Jose Napoles. Future Hall of Famer Napoles was heavily favored, but Muniz did everything but go home with the crown. Napoles was declared the winner by technical draw in what every boxing authority says was one of the biggest robberies in pugilistic history. Muniz had a few more shots at the title, but came up short against Carlos Palomino. He retired after a loss to Sugar Ray Leonard. He never came back, even though he told me that there were plenty of offers to fight young and up-and-comers, like he had once been. Big money was offered, but Muniz knew he was finished. He didn't want to be a punching bag. I lost track of Muniz after his retirement. I later learned he taught Spanish and coached wrestling at a high school in Southern California. One day I sent him an email that led to our ongoing friendship.

As much as I admired Muhammad Ali, Muniz is my all-time favorite fighter. His aggressive style, never-say-die attitude, and professionalism, are all great traits. But most of all, Armando Muniz is a very nice guy. He looks out for his fellow man.

Matthew Saad Muhammad: I first knew him as Matthew Franklin. He was Philadelphia tough and a can't-miss action fighter. He was fighting Marvin Johnson. Actually, battling is a more fitting word. Back and forth the fight went with blood and guts in equal display. Johnson appeared to be in control, until almost getting knocked out in round four. Franklin's eye was closing, but he finally caught and stopped Johnson in round 12. He would be in a number of "edge of doom" brawls over the next five years.

I remember watching a program that relayed the story of Franklin being dropped at the Benjamin Franklin Parkway in Philadelphia in 1958. He was four years old. He thought a family member would claim him. Nobody did. He was taken in by Catholic Social Services where a nun named him Matthew Franklin. A few years later, Franklin was adopted by a Portuguese family. His neighborhood was tough and he joined a gang. Sent to reform school, Franklin found his calling when a kindly counselor introduced him to boxing. After a short amateur career, Franklin turned professional.

Twelve fights into his pro career, he fought future champions Mate Parlov, and Marvin Camel, back-to-back, and beat them both. Franklin was a fan-friendly fighter-never in a dull fight. After his dramatic stoppage of Johnson, he defeated Billy Douglas, and Richie Kates, and stopped perennial contender Yaqui Lopez. A shot at a world title was on the horizon. All he had to do was defeat Johnson again, this time in Indianapolis. The fight was telecast live on CBS. Johnson appeared to have the edge through seven give-and-take rounds. Franklin was bleeding, but unloading. Johnson went for broke in the eighth – but was caught and floored by a wicked Franklin hook. The brave warrior got up, but the referee waved the fight off. Franklin was the new WBC light heavyweight champion. After the fight, he changed his name to Matthew Saad Muhammad. He defended his title against classy John Conteh twice, and Louis Pergaud, before facing Lopez in a rematch. The fight was all about blood and guts. Each hammered each other viciously until Saad Muhammad took over later in the fight. Saad Muhammad successfully defended his title four more times until facing Dwight Braxton.

Braxton, who eventually changed his named to Dwight Muhammad Quai, was focused and ready. Like a bull in a boxing ring, he stalked and battered Saad Muhammad. The soon-to-be ex-champion was finally facing a foe he couldn't rally against. He hung in as long as he could, until a knockdown in round 10 convinced the referee the fight was over. A rematch six months later was a one-sided beatdown. Saad Muhammad was only 27, but finished as a top-notch boxer. The life and death battles had caught up with him.

He would fight on for another 10 years, losing more than he won-a mere shadow of what he once was. Seeing him lose to fighters who, a few years before couldn't have carried his jock, was tough. I could only imagine how he felt. A number of years later, I read that he was broke and living in a shelter.

I could only shake my head. This kind of rags to riches to rags story is very common in boxing. Fighters attract vampires they can't trust, only to be sucked dry and discarded. Saad Muhammad died in 2014. He was 59. Cause of death was amyotrophic lateral sclerosis, also known as Lou Gehrig's disease. It's not surprising that in the end, his huge heart was still fighting.

The last fighter on my list actually broke my heart in 1977. **Carlos Palomino** was, altering a quote and changing a word from the movie *Predator,* one tough mofu. My grandfather told me about Palomino in 1973. Said he'd one day be a champ. I think I grunted. I was following Armando Muniz, who fought in the same division (welterweight) as Palomino. I started paying closer attention to Palomino after my phone call with Grandpa.

In 1974, he lost his first fight to Andy "The Hawk" Price. No disgrace there. As it was in those days, two months later he was in a do-or-die fight with Nelson Ruiz. Ruiz was no slouch. He'd been in the ring with contender Felipe Vaca, and former champion Eddie Perkins. Palomino battered Ruiz, winning by stoppage in round six. He wouldn't lose again for five years. Palomino had to get past upset-minded Zovek Barajas to ensure bigger fights. It wasn't easy. Their first fight, a classic barn-burner at the Olympic Auditorium, was judged a draw. A little over a month later, Palomino met Barajas again. Palomino broke Barajas and stopped him in nine. After a draw against Hedgemon Lewis, Palomino was in line for a title shot against new champion John H. Stracey of London. Instead he took step-aside money to let Lewis fight Stracey. Palomino was ringside to watch Stracey defeat Lewis in 10. His chance against Stracey came three months later, again in England. Palomino entered the fight a 10-1 underdog.

Stracey was riding high after winning the title from long-time champion Jose Napoles, and defending it with a crushing stoppage of Lewis. His promoter figured Palomino was easy pickings. The British media was even predicting in which round the fight would end. Problem was, Palomino had seen something in Stracey's style he hoped to exploit. His strategy (bodyshots) worked perfectly. Stracey fought well, but Palomino grew stronger as the fight progressed. His left hook to the gut softened up the champion. In the 12th round, a perfect left hook to Stracey's liver ended the fight. Palomino was a champ. I was happy. "King Carlos" carried himself with dignity. I knew though that a showdown with Muniz would have to happen. It did in 1977.

Palomino rose from a first round knockdown to stop Muniz in the 15th round. He defended his title six more times before losing it by majority decision to Wilfred Benitez in 1979. I was shocked when he retired less than a year later. He appeared in some wildly popular beer commercials in the 80s and 90s. Then he did it again. He shocked the boxing world by coming out of retirement at 47. He did it for his father, who had recently passed away. He went 4-1 in his comeback. One of his wins was over two-time world champion, Rene Arredondo. The Olympic was sold-out when

Palomino fought high-ranking contender Wilfred Rivera in 1997. Twenty years removed from his world title, Palomino fought hard, but lost by decision.

He retired again after the fight. I was honored to help induct Palomino into The West Coast Boxing Hall of Fame in 2015. The moment was surreal.

I reminded Palomino before I took the stage that he had broken my heart in 1977. He looked at me and said, "Really?" I nodded and smiled. What a fighter.

It Ain't Over Till It's Over

By Jerry Fitch

Throughout the years there have been more than a few classic boxing matches that resulted in sudden endings that snatched victory from defeat for the eventual winner. In this chapter I recall six of the most famous ones, two of which were included in chapters of my book *My Favorite Fights*. (REaD CORNER 2018)

Joe Louis-Billy Conn I, June 18, 1941, New York. This particular fight is one of the classics that so many people discuss till this day. Fans have talked about it and re-lived it over and over again. There have been many theories as to why it ended the way it did.

Billy Conn the World Light-heavyweight Champion moved up to challenge several heavyweight contenders in 1940, eventually relinquishing his light-heavy title in May of 1941. By then he had defeated Bob Pastor, Al McCoy, Lee Savold and Buddy Knox.

Never really a heavyweight in stature Billy had his sights set on the heavyweight crown worn by Joe Louis. Billy was flamboyant, confident and had a big following of not only Pittsburgh fans but many other fans nationwide. His brash attitude made him a favorite of the Irish-American fans too. He was cocky yes, but he had the ability to back it up.

Joe Louis and Billy Conn were signed to fight on June 18, 1941 in New York at the Polo Grounds. There are many stories about the actual weight of Billy Conn entering the fight that night. On the official records it is listed as 174 lbs. Joe Louis was just under 200 lbs. However Billy Conn was said to have only weighed 169 lbs. Mike Jacobs, the promoter somehow fudged the weight fearing there would be an outcry if Conn got badly beaten at such a weight disadvantage. What I can say about the weight is that Billy Conn told me face-to-face in 1981 that he indeed only weighed 169 lbs.

The fight itself was a beauty. Billy Conn showed no fear as he put on a boxing clinic and appeared to be on his way to victory. He boxed smartly and used his speed and boxing skills to keep Louis off stride. In the 12th round Conn staggered the champion and after the bell he went back to his corner full of confidence that he was on his way to become the heavyweight champion.

Of course in the 13th round Billy made the mistake of continuing his assault on Joe Louis. There are varying stories as to what his corner said to him prior to the start of the round. One version is that Billy told them he was going to knock Louis out and they pleaded with him to be smart, to box, not take any chances.

Everyone knows how this fight ended. With seconds left in the 13th round Louis caught Billy with a devastating uppercut and a series of punches that put him on the canvas where he struggled to get up but couldn't make it. The time was 2:58 seconds of the round.

The biggest misconception of this fight always seems to be when people try to say Billy Conn had the fight won and all he had to do was stay on his feet till the end. If Billy had been smart and stayed away perhaps he could have won a decision, then again maybe not. However the scoring entering the fateful 13th round had Billy Conn winning 7-4, 7-5 with the third score being even at 6-6. Obviously he still could have lost the fight by decision. People tend to forget that fact.

Most articles have Billy telling everyone after the fight "what was the sense of being Irish if you are not stupid," or words similar to that. On the video after the fight Billy is heard saying, "I guess I had too much to win for tonight. Otherwise I would have won easy." I asked him about that and he told me he had visited his very ill mother prior to the fight and told her "Ma the next time you see me I am going to be heavyweight champion of the world."

Jake LaMotta-Laurent Dauthuille, September 13, 1950, Detroit, Michigan. This bout was the classic example of "It Ain't Over Till It's Over."

Jake LaMotta was defending his middleweight title for the second time when he met the Frenchman, Laurent Dauthuille. In the previous year Dauthuille had won a unanimous decision over LaMotta with slick boxing skills. That fight took place in Montreal where Dauthuille had taken as his home base after moving from France.

Dauthuille was a worthy challenger but nobody expected him to completely dominate the champion and build up a substantial lead like he did. He boxed in and out of range and LaMotta never seemed to be able to put together a series of punches. The title was rapidly slipping away from LaMotta. Entering the final round Jake appeared spent.

More than a few times in his career Jake LaMotta played possum. Entering the 15th round perhaps he was trying to lull his challenger into a false sense of security and obviously it worked, whether planned or not. With seconds remaining in the fight LaMotta launched a barrage of punches that the Frenchman couldn't seem to avoid. With only 13 seconds left in the fight Jake threw a looping left which landed solidly on the Frenchman's jaw and sent him crashing to the canvas, where he was counted out.

The scoring at the time of the knockout was all Dauthuille, 72-68, 74-66, 71-69. In other words Dauthuille had the fight in the bag. Although Dauthuille had fifteen more fights in his career, after this fight he never again fought for the title.

The LaMotta-Dauthuille fight of 1950 was named *The Ring* magazine's Fight of the Year.

Joey Maxim-Sugar Ray Robinson, June 25, 1952, New York. This fight will forever go down in boxing history as the only time the great Sugar Ray Robinson failed to go the distance in a fight. The circumstances were unusual for several reasons.

Originally the fight was to be held on June 23rd but a torrential rainstorm forced a postponement. The rescheduled date on June

25th at Yankee Stadium turned out to be one of the hottest days ever recorded in New York City.

This bout was the second defense of Joey Maxim's light-heavyweight title that he had won against Freddie Mills on January 24, 1950, in London, England. He successfully defended his title in August of 1951 in a thrilling fight against "Irish" Bob Murphy over fifteen rounds in New York's Madison Square Garden. He won unanimously with scores of 10-3, 10-5 and 10-5.

Sugar Ray Robinson was seeking his third title having held the welterweight title and the middleweight title twice. At the time of his title challenge against Maxim he was still the reigning middleweight kingpin. Entering the fight Robinson had fought 137 times and had lost only two fights in his career.

The heat on the night of the fight was said to be anywhere from 104 to 105 degrees at ringside. Anyone sitting ringside in that stifling heat would suffer greatly. Moving around in a boxing ring under the lights and expending energy would be beyond comprehension even for a well conditioned athlete.

Though Joey Maxim was not a knockout puncher he was the bigger man by far and had a lot of boxing skills. Besides an excellent jab and a granite jaw, Joey knew how to force clinches and lean on an opponent. He knew every trick in the trade and his history as a rugged fighter was beyond question. When a man fights as many great fighters and big punchers as Joey did and only was stopped once in 115 professional fights, well, that says it all. To top it off Joey Maxim weighed 174 ¾ pounds and Sugar Ray was only 157 ½. Robinson had also lost a few pounds after the fight was postponed and rescheduled.

The only way Sugar Ray was going to defeat Joey Maxim was by using his speed and out-boxing him. So he did, he moved around the ring and fought a smart fight, using his skills the best way he knew how. However as each round went along Robinson was expending a lot of energy. For ten rounds he was doing it right, he was winning without a doubt. But he was doing most of the

123

movement while Maxim was content to counter and tie his man up. Maxim let Robinson do most of the work.

After ten rounds there was no doubt who was winning. The heat took the first casualty of the evening when referee Ruby Goldstein collapsed and had to be replaced by Ray Miller after the 10th round.

Although Robinson won the 11th and 12th rounds and landed some big punches, Maxim started to land some good hooks to the body himself. The spring was going out of Robinson's legs and he barely made it back to his corner as he flopped onto his stool as the 12th round ended. His seconds worked on him with water and smelling salts but that only brought minimal relief.

As the 13th round began it was obvious Sugar Ray was moving slowly and punches that Maxim couldn't land in the earlier rounds were now landing with ease. The punches weren't any harder than they had been earlier but now they were taking their toll. Robinson swung in desperation with a couple wild right hands and the second one missed so badly that he fell flat on his face. Apparently that took all of the remaining strength out of his body. When he got up Maxim hit him with a few more punches along the ropes that staggered him. The bell is the only thing that saved Robinson from going down again.

Sugar Ray's trainer Harry Wiley and second Peewee Beal had to carry him back to his corner. Dr. Alexander Schiff, commission physician, came into the ring and it was obvious Sugar Ray had gone as far as he could go. When the bell sounded for round fourteen, Robinson could not come out.

Sugar Ray was in front by the scores of 10-3, 9-3-1 and 7-3-3 when the fight was halted giving Maxim a 14th round TKO win. It was a heroic effort by Robinson and maybe on another night without the heat he would have been able to finish what he had started.

Over the years I spent time with Joey Maxim in Cleveland and at a few boxing dinners in other states. The subject of the Robinson fight always seemed to come up. More times than not the fact the heat did Robinson in that night in 1952 was talked about over and over. Joey Maxim felt he was not given any credit for fighting a very smart fight. It was a source of irritation for Joey and his usual reply was, "What did everyone think I was fighting in air-conditioning that night?"

Jersey Joe Walcott-Rocky Marciano I, September 23, 1952, Philadelphia. This fight has always been one of my all-time favorites. I have watched it countless times over the years.

Personally I think it is one of the best heavyweight championship fights ever.

Jersey Joe Walcott won the heavyweight championship on his fifth try. He will always be one of the best examples of a person who never gave up no matter what the odds were. At the time of his victory over Ezzard Charles on July 18, 1951 in Pittsburgh, by a one punch 7th round knockout, Jersey Joe was 37 years old. The fans of today might look at someone that age as being young. Back in the era that Jersey Joe Walcott fought he was considered old in boxing terms. At the time of his victory and for many years after he was the oldest man to ever win the heavyweight title. Jersey Joe was referred to at various times as "old man Walcott" or "Pappy Joe."

Before the fight Jersey Joe Walcott dismissed Marciano as lacking the ability to defeat him. Jersey Joe considered him unschooled and without finesse. "Write this down," he growled to reporters. "He can't fight. If I don't lick him, take my name out of the record books."

When the bell rang for the first round it was obvious Jersey Joe believed what he had said as he tore into Marciano and eventually floored him with a nifty left hook. Marciano was up at four but took a pounding the rest of the round. It set the tone for the fight. Most of the battle was give and take but Jersey Joe was giving more than he was taking. Both men were cut and hit with solid punches throughout. People who have been accustomed to watching two big guys walk around and pose half of the time in many heavyweight fights must have been thrilled to see this fight live.

Walcott had the upper edge in the first three rounds with Marciano coming back into the fight in the next few rounds. An apparent clash of heads in the 6th round caused a gash over Walcott's eye and a cut on Marciano's scalp. Both corners applied something to stop the bleeding and after the 7th round Marciano complained he couldn't see.

Something had gotten into Marciano's eyes that impaired his vision and for the next three rounds Walcott took full advantage of it. He battered Marciano and opened more cuts and raised some swelling. Marciano's corner accused Walcott's handlers of foul play saying they felt Walcott's corner had put some sort of liniment on Jersey Joe's shoulders which was transferred to Marciano's eyes in a clinch. It was never proven.

This story of the liniment getting into the eyes reminds me of the similar situation when the then Cassius Clay fought Sonny Liston in their first fight. Clay was blinded for a couple rounds. Angelo Dundee and Clay's corner accused Liston's corner of foul play.

The remaining rounds of the Walcott-Marciano fight were filled with action as Jersey Joe continued to build on his lead. When the bell sounded ending the 12th round, Walcott was ahead on all three scorecards; 7-4, 7-5, 8-4. All Jersey Joe had to do was stay on his feet and finish the fight to hold onto his title. Marciano's only chance was to win by a knockout and that is just what he did. Early in the round Walcott backed into the ropes as Marciano crouched and came forward. Then as both men started to throw right hands Marciano's "Suzy Q" landed first and it was lights out for Jersey Joe. The time was 43 seconds of the 13th round and the end of Jersey Joe Walcott's reign as heavyweight champion.

Ruben Olivares-Alexis Arguello, November 23, 1974, Inglewood, California. I became a fan of Ruben Olivares after reading about him in various boxing magazines in the late 1960s. Before that I had witnessed several Mexican fighters in action while I was in the Army stationed in Oklahoma. We would get tape-delay fights that were held the previous Thursday from the Olympic Auditorium in Los Angeles. This is when I really learned how exciting Mexican battlers could be.

It was easy to become aware of Ruben Olivares after he started fighting outside of his native Mexico and began making a big name for himself in California. He was known as "Rockabye Ruben" because of his knockout power. He thrilled fans both north and south of the border as he went undefeated from 1964 to 1969. Eventually he won the World Bantamweight Championship from Lionel Rose on August 22, 1969, by a 5th round knockout.

The next few years were a roller coaster ride for Ruben Olivares. He defended his title twice, then lost it by a kayo to Chucho Castillo in October of 1970, won it back from Castillo in April of 1971. Olivares then defended his newly won title twice against Kazuyoshi Kanazawa and Jesus Pimentel in October and December of 1971, winning both by knockouts.

Ruben promptly lost his title again on March 19, 1972 to Rafael Herrera via an 8th round knockout. The word in boxing circles was that Olivares spent too much time partying and not training. Sometimes he was not in tiptop shape when he came into the ring and although he had the fire power to win most any fight, it didn't always work out that way.

In June of 1973 Ruben won the vacant NABF Featherweight Title by stopping Bobby Chacon in the 9th round by a TKO. He defended that title against Art Hafey, then was given a shot at the vacant WBA Featherweight Title against Zensuke Utagawa on July 9, 1974 at the Forum in Inglewood, California. He won the title with a 7th round knockout, the 66th of his career.

This brings us to Olivares' title defense against Alexis Arguello on November 23, 1974, also in Inglewood. This turned out to be an amazing fight also. I will admit at the time I didn't have much of a clue as to who Alexis Arguello was or how good he might be.

Alexis Arguello was from Managus, Nicaragua. From 1968 until he met Ruben Olivares for the title in 1974 he had fought a total of 42 fights and the only time he fought outside of his native Nicaragua was in a failed attempt to win the WBA Featherweight Title against Ernesto Marcel on February 16, 1974 in Panama City, Panama. He lost a 15-round decision in that bid.

So when Ruben Olivares and Alexis Arguello were signed to fight I simply felt Olivares would defend his title easily. I knew very little about the man who would eventually be called "The Explosive Thin Man." I had to go with the champion.

The title fight went off as scheduled on November 23, 1974 in Inglewood and it was apparent Ruben Olivares had taken Alexis Arguello seriously because he seemed in very fine shape. Olivares put on a good performance for twelve rounds with both men landing heavy leather. After Olivares took a knee-buckling hook in the opening round he was dominating Arguello for the next three rounds before getting careless in the 5th round. He then took back command of the fight starting in the 6th round.

Olivares was not just a headhunter as he landed paralyzing shots to Arguello's liver during the fight. Olivares had Arguello in very bad shape in the 12th round. Fans were in a frenzy and many observers wondered if Arguello would even be able to come out for the 13th round.

The 13th round is where I became fully aware of just how devastating a puncher Arguello could be. Ruben Olivares was one of the great finishers when he had a man hurt and apparently he felt Arguello was ready to go. He jumped right into the attack but suddenly Alexis Arguello landed a perfect left hook that met Ruben's jaw straight on. Olivares was dazed and on his hands and knees as he spit out his mouthpiece. He managed to beat the count. A later review showed it took referee Dick Young nearly 25 seconds before the fighters were able to resume fighting. It didn't matter however. Arguello launched another left hook not nearly as good as the first one, but it dropped Olivares once again and this time he did not get up.

At the time of the knockout Olivares was leading by scores of 8-3, 6-4 and 7-4. After this fight I did not suddenly stop being an Olivares fan. However I was now an Arguello fan also and followed him throughout the rest of his career.

John Tate-Mike Weaver, March 31, 1980, Knoxville, Tennessee. This is not only another fight with a surprising finish, it also was a career changing bout. John Tate had a very good amateur career and won a Bronze Medal in the 1976 Summer Olympics in the heavyweight division.

John Tate's career as a professional started in 1977 and was meteoric. Big John as he was known in boxing circles met every challenge. Among his victims were Bernardo Mercado, Johnny Boudreaux, Cookie Wallace, Duane Bobick and Kalie Knoetze as he cruised to a 19-0 record with 16 kayo wins. Then on October 20, 1979 he met South Africa's Gerrie Coetzee for the vacant WBA Heavyweight Title in Pretoria, South Africa, during the height of apartheid.

The Tate-Coetzee fight was watched by 81,000 mostly white fans. The ring was wet from the rain and several times both fighters slipped. However the wet canvas mainly seemed to cause Coetzee more problems. Once after stunning Tate with a left hand, he moved in to throw his "bionic right" and slipped and lost his balance before he could get it off.

John Tate fought a very good fight and won a unanimous decision over the South African hopeful who was undefeated heading into this championship fight with a record of 22-0. Coetzee had defeated some big-name fighters leading up to this fight including Ron Stander, Mike Schutte, Kallie Knoetze, Randy Stephens and Leon Spinks whom he knocked out in the first round on June 24, 1979 in Monte Carlo.

So John Tate was now heavyweight champion of the world and it seemed there would be no stopping him. His career had gone along perfectly as planned and there was no telling how much more he could possibly accomplish. Or so it seemed at the time.

John Tate was then signed to defend his newly won crown on March 31, 1980 in his adopted hometown of Knoxville, Tennessee against Mike Weaver. The previous year Weaver had put up a heroic battle against Larry Holmes in quest of Holmes' WBC Heavyweight Title before being stopped in the 12th round. However Weaver's record was spotty at best and was sprinkled with nine losses, five of them by knockout including the Holmes defeat. Mike Weaver had lost to Larry Frazier and Duane Bobick by knockout and had lost decisions to Stan Ward and Leroy Jones.

Big John Tate towered over Mike Weaver and outweighed him 232 lbs. to 207 ½. He used his size advantage in this fight and boxed well. After the fight Weaver remarked that Tate "was strong, very agile and he moved pretty good." "He was out-boxing me and out maneuvering me. I was tight, my manager and trainer were yelling 'Throw more punches.'"

Weaver was behind but finally started to do some damage in the 12th round. He hurt Tate and sent him reeling. For some reason Weaver didn't press the attack in the 13th round and to add insult to injury he also lost a point in the 14th round because of a low blow. Weaver did however wobble Tate with a left hook as the 14th round was coming to an end.

Heading into the last round Weaver trailed by scores of 138-133, 137-134 and 136-133. I am sure he knew he was losing and that he had to stop Tate or otherwise suffer his 10th career loss. With less than a minute to go in the round Weaver pinned Tate on the ropes. Tate tried to shove Weaver away but was met with a return shove that caused him to bounce into the ropes. Weaver dug a right into Tate's body and then uncorked a short left hook that exploded off the champion's face. For all practical purposes Tate was out already but Weaver made sure of it as he landed a final right that sent Tate crashing face down like a giant oak tree, out before he even hit the canvas. The time was 2:15 of the round. I watched this fight live and I was as shocked at the finish as everyone else probably was at the time.

That one fight had changed the direction of John Tate's career and his life. In his next fight he was stopped by Trevor Berbick in the 9th round. He did win some fights after that but never contended for the championship again. He retired in 1988 after losing a decision to Noel Quarless. His final record was 37-3.

John Tate's life after retirement was filled with health and personal problems. It was reported he was hooked on drugs. He was also arrested twice for petty theft and assault, in and out of jail for probation violations.

On April 9, 1998 John Tate died in Knoxville when he lost control of his pick-up truck on an entrance ramp to an interstate highway. The accident may have been caused by a stroke. He had been diagnosed with a brain tumor. John was only 43 years old.

Five Must See Boxing Movies

By John J. Raspanti

I can still hear my Dad's voice 55 years later. "John! Come in here. You have to see this!" I raced to the family room where Dad was on the couch watching television. He smiled as he said, "Watch this." I did, although I wasn't quite sure what I was watching. It had a gritty feel and looked realistic.

Dad told me the film was called *Body and Soul* and the star was John Garfield. We watched the last 15 minutes of the movie. It took me years until I was able to see the entire film. It didn't matter. The movie and its star made an impression on me.

Boxing and the movies have coexisted for over 100 years. Charlie Chaplin made a film called *The Ring* in 1914. It was a Chaplin film, so the movie was a hit. Not all were. Many failed. The 1940s and 50s were a glorious time for boxing movies. This was the period Dad introduced me to. They were his films, the ones he watched growing up. Even my mom would sometimes wander into the living room and say, "I remember that one," as Dad and I watched the screen.

The following is a list of what I consider the best five, and most important, fistic films. Thought I loved both of them, *Rocky* and *Raging Bull* don't appear on the list. To me, it's the older films that capture the feel of the wicked and brutal world of the red-light sport.

Let's start with the aforementioned *Body and Soul*. When John Garfield decided to make the movie in 1947, a few standards were already in place. The hero was a great guy. He'd always do the right thing, win the fight--and the girl. Garfield's film changed that. Garfield, who boxed in his teens, had long wanted to make a boxing movie. The sport had always been a personal favorite. He played a pugilist in *They Made a Criminal* in 1939, and Warner Brothers had been on the lookout for a feature for years. Garfield's rise to film stardom resembled that of an unknown boxer climbing the rankings and becoming a champion.

He grew up (born Jacob Jules Garfinkle in 1913) poor on the rough and tumble streets of New York's Lower East Side. Garfield joined a gang, ditched school, and engaged in street fights. His life had little purpose until he was shipped off to a school for troubled children. There he discovered acting and was encouraged by the man who ran the school, Angelo Patri. A number of years later he said this about Patri. "He (Patri) reached into the garbage can and pulled me out, I owe him everything."

Garfield made his debut on Broadway in 1931. Several years later, he was part of an elite pack of actors called "The Group," run by Lee Strasberg. Garfield's friend, playwright Clifford Odets, wrote "Golden Boy" in 1937 to star Garfield, but the role went to another actor. The consensus was that Garfield wasn't experienced enough to handle the lead. The play opened in November 1937, with Garfield playing a minor role, and was a smash hit. Garfield felt the sting of discontent and bitterness. Officials from Warner Brothers and MGM, who had seen him on stage, contacted him; they wanted him to take a screen test.

A few weeks after the test, both studios offered contracts. Garfield signed with Warner's, a two-picture deal that would be completed within a year. His first film was *Four Daughters*, a tearjerker about four sisters and their father. The film was completed quickly and Garfield moved on to his second picture. Jack Warner convinced him to change his name from Jules Garfinkle to John Garfield. He completed his work for Warner Brothers and went home, figuring that was the last he would hear from the studio.

The success of *Four Daughters* made Garfield a star. His natural acting style was unlike that of most screen stars of the time. For the next seven years, he starred or co-starred in a number of box office hits. Still, even though he had played a boxer in "They Made Me a Criminal," his ambitions went unfulfilled.

That changed in 1946 when Garfield formed his own film company and bought the rights to the story of war hero, and former world champion, Barney Ross, who battled and defeated a drug problem. The project went nowhere until Garfield met with writer Abraham Polansky. Getting Ross' film made was problematical, so Polansky pitched some changes to the story. Garfield liked what he heard. The working title for the film was *Body and Soul*.

The title represents the internal battle fought by the main character, Charlie Davis, played by Garfield, throughout the film. Fame and fortune symbolized the body, while friendship and love the soul. Davis tries to balance these opposing forces, fully aware of the consequences. The movie is set during the Great Depression. Finding work is nearly impossible. Davis a poor kid living in the slums, gets a taste of success when he wins an amateur boxing tournament. He wants to fight, but his mother is firmly against it.

The support of his girlfriend Peg (played by Lilli Palmer) changes everything. After the senseless death of his father, Davis ls left with few options. His mother's failed attempt at financial relief enrages him. The dye has been cast. "Get me that fight from Quinn," Davis yells at his friend Shorty. "I want money. Do you understand? Money, money!"

Davis turns professional and racks up 21 consecutive wins. He's a natural fighter, but his demons are also in play, greed being one of them. To get a shot at the champion, Davis will have to make a deal. The dealmaker is an icy mobster named Roberts (played by Lloyd Gough) who smells big money. Davis' best friend warns him to stay away from Roberts. Davis listens, but ignores the advice. Roberts sweetens the deal by giving Davis an envelope overflowing with cash. Davis, always a little rough round the edges, grows more ruthless. His relationships suffer. He wins the title, but isn't aware that the champion (Canada Lee) is suffering from a blood clot. The battering he takes from Davis almost kills him. Davis learns the truth, but after achieving his dream of becoming a champion, refuses to walk away. He's the champ, but in the process, he loses his best friend, who dies, and his loving girlfriend. Davis lives high and spends lavishly. His new girl is a manipulative floozy. Still the money is rolling in and out. Until it isn't.

The day of reckoning finally comes when Davis visits Roberts's office to collect another advance, but this time the mobster turns him down. Roberts tells Davis he needs to box again, but he'll also have to do Roberts a favor. He'll fight a young undefeated hot shot, and – he'll lose. Davis reunites with his level-headed girlfriend. He eventually explains to her, and his mother, what he's up against. "There's a million bucks riding on my back," he says. "If I don't fight, I don't get a dime. I'm all mobbed up, tied hand and foot, down to my last buck." The climatic fight scene, unrelenting and gritty, is a mixed bag of betrayal and revenge. Cinematographer James Wong Howe filmed the boxing scenes while on roller skates to add realism.

Garfield earned a well-deserved Academy Award nomination for his portrayal of Davis. His acting is edgy and charismatic. His intensity carries the film. Canada Lee, who played his trainer Ben, is also outstanding. His scenes with Garfield are wonderful. Even today, *Body and Soul* is relevant. The film resounds as a warning of the corruption that lingers on the edges of "The Sweet Science" - ready to pounce and wreak havoc on the ambitious.

Next is *The Set-Up*, shot two years after *Body and Soul*. The movie has many admirers, including Academy Award directors Martin Scorsese and Billy Wilder. An argument can be made that it's the best boxing film ever made. It's that good. The concept was born from the body of a poem, penned by Joseph Mancure in 1947. Former sports writer and boxing fan Art Cohn wrote the screenplay, replacing stereotypes and adding racial diversity, but left in the "set-up" and many of the unscrupulous characters.

Chosen to direct was Robert Wise. Wise was talented. He began his career in the sound department at RKO before being promoted to editor in 1939. Two years later, he edited a little movie called *Citizen Kane*, earning an Oscar nomination. That was fine, but Wise was chomping at the bit to direct. He finally got his chance in 1944. He scored an immediate success with *The Curse of the Cat People*.

Character actor Robert Ryan was offered the starring role in *The Set-Up*. Ryan played minor roles until his breakthrough performance in the 1947 film noir classic, *Crossfire*. His villainous portrayal of a racist character was so believable that many of the following roles he was offered were similar to the character he had already played. Ryan was hungry for something different. When offered *The Set-Up*, he accepted eagerly. It didn't hurt that Ryan had boxed while attending Dartmouth College, being crowned the heavyweight champion for four consecutive years. His skills brought realism to the boxing scenes. The film, told in real time (72 mins) relates the story of journeyman boxer, Bill "Stoker" Thompson. Stoker is 35, an old man in the boxing ring, but outside it, he still dreams of getting one more shot at the big time. He tells his wife (Audrey Totter, in a tender performance) that he's only "one punch away." She gently reminds him that he's been saying that for years. She wants him to quit, and refuses to go to the arena and see him get his brains scrambled. Stoker is crestfallen. He doesn't want to quit. He can still punch. He tells her he's going to win.

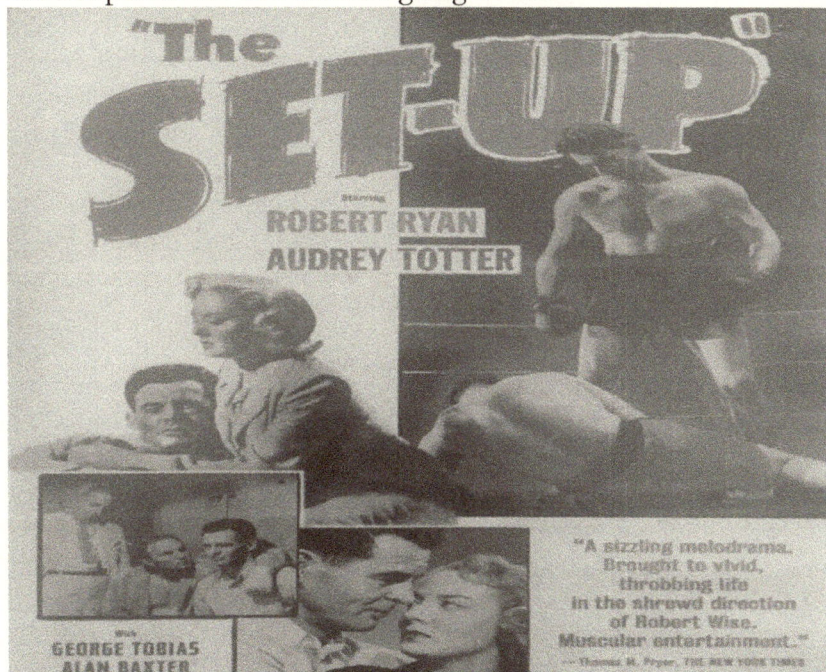

His opponent is a mobbed-up fighter named Tiger Nelson. The kid is undefeated, and something of a heartthrob. Stoker doesn't know that his weasel manager Tiny (George Tobias) and slimy cutman Red (Percy Helton) have already made a deal with Nelson's manager for Stoker to lose. They keep this information to themselves, figuring the old man doesn't have a chance to win anyway. Stoker has other ideas. Later in the film, we see Stoker at the arena in a crowded dressing room. He watches as the other fighters go into battle, some winning, others losing, as he reflects on the peaks and valleys of his long career.

Stoker is worried about his wife, who's depressed and wandering the dark streets of the city, pondering what to do. She loves Stoker, but can't bear the thought of seeing him brutalized. The climatic fight, set in a smoke-filled arena, is a beautifully shot potpourri of guts, pride, and betrayal. The cinematography, by Milton R. Krasner, is superb. The tight shots bring the viewer into the action. It's brutal and bloody. Director Wise cuts to members of the blood-thirsty audience--a woman who complains each time the referee breaks up the fighters; a blind man who enjoys hearing about the violence; another man throwing punches at the air. The quick cutting from the fight to the frenzied fans creates a mood of both disgust and despair. Stoker hangs tough against his young opponent. Between rounds, he searches the audience, hoping to catch a glimpse of his wife. His manager is finally told that he needs to lie down. He argues he can take the kid, but it doesn't matter what he's told. He'll have to lose. but how does he do that? This is his dream, but if he wins, he could end up in an alley with a bullet in his back.

Ryan is fantastic as Stoker. He's tough, but kind, and loaded with decency. He's skilled at showing emotion with his eyes. When he talks about being "one punch away," they light up and sparkle. But later, as he gazes at the hotel where his wife is, or at the empty seat he bought for her in the arena, despair, and a quiet despondence creep in. He's the tragic hero. It's impossible not to cheer for him. *The Set-Up* is a brilliant film, filled with grit and depth. Stoker is a man desperate to prove himself. He's searching for redemption. He's been battered and knocked down, but he won't give up. All he's trying to do is survive.

Rocky Graziano retired from boxing in 1952. He was either 33 or 30, depending on who you ask. Nobody ever called him a great fighter. But that didn't matter. He was wildly popular, extremely gutsy, hit like a mule, and once was the middleweight champion of the world. His rise to the title was about as unlikely as a homeless bum becoming a world champion. Apparently, for entertainment purposes, Graziano's father, a former fighter, abused him and made him box his older brother. He was three.

Ultimately, this brutality helped when he fought. Which was often. He was intense, hated his opponents, and had a hair-trigger temper. He wanted to kill them. He seethed rage. As a teenager, he fought, stole, violated his parole and landed in reform school. The future looked bleak until he won the Metropolitan amateur welterweight tournament. He promptly went out and hocked the medal he won for $15 dollars. It was likely he was told to turn professional, but didn't. Training bored him. It took discipline.

He eventually went pro. Five years later, after going AWOL from the U.S. Army and serving a year in jail, he won the middleweight championship of the world by stopping tough Tony Zale. His story reads like a fable. Hollywood agreed. When Graziano (with the help of Rowland Barber) penned his autobiography in 1955, Tinseltown immediately bought the rights. *Somebody Up There Likes Me* was made a year later.

The film starred Paul Newman, whose career was teetering after his debut in *The Silver Chalice*. The producer's original choice, James Dean, was killed in an automobile accident a few weeks before production was to start. Dean had talked to Graziano on the phone before he died. He wanted to go to New York and observe the former champ. After Dean's death, Newman, who had replaced Dean in a television adaptation of Ernest Hemingway's *The Battler* a few months before, was selected to play Graziano. Newman went to New York and hung out with Graziano for a few months. They bonded. Newman picked up some of Graziano's mannerisms. The pressure was on. Newman had auditioned against Dean for the lead role in *East of Eden* the year before. Dean got the role. Many doubted Newman could pull off the difficult part. In this writer's opinion, it's hard to imagine anyone, including Dean, delivering a better performance.

Robert Wise returned to the boxing ring to direct *Somebody Up There Likes Me*. He wanted authenticity, so he shot the film on the city streets where the young Graziano prowled. The screenplay, by Ernest Lehman, closely follows the book. Graziano's eventual rise from delinquency and crime, mixing with gangsters, coming to grips with his past, and belief in himself, are wonderfully depicted. Newman's performance is a mix of anger, fear, and humor. Newman captues a Graziano who is both charismatic and likeable. The film also shows the darker side of Graziano's life. The acting by all is first rate. Everett Sloan is excellent as Graziano's loyal manager, while Eileen Heckart is touching as "Ma" Graziano. Sal Mineo, wo co-starred in Dean's *Rebel Without a Cause* in 1955, brings gravitas to his small role as Graziano's loyal friend. Pier Angeli is sweet and tough as Graziano's supportive wife, Norma. The boxing scenes are well done. Numerous closeups add suspense. Newman is believable enough in the squared circle that even most boxing purists won't groan. The dramatic re-creation of Graziano winning the middleweight title is exciting and brutal. The real Zale and Graziano knew no other way to fight. Their three fights will live forever. The movie captures the heart of both.

A year later, another movie based on a real fighter was released. If *Somebody Up There Likes Me* was a mixture of "dark and light," *The*

Harder They Fall was mostly dark. The story, based on Budd
Schulberg's novel of the same name, is loosely based on real-life
boxer Primo Carnera. The story concerns unemployed sportswriter
Eddie Willis (Humphrey Bogart in his last screen role) getting
caught up in the unscrupulous dealings of mobster Nick Benko
(Rod Steiger) as he attempts to "create" a heavyweight contender.
Willis is desperate. He hasn't worked for months. He's pushing
60 and feeling it. "A guy past his forties shouldn't have to run
anymore," he tells Benko. Benko offers Willis a job and major
money as a press agent for a big heavyweight fighter from
Argentina. The guy is six-foot-eight and undefeated, says Benko.

The opening scenes, shot in Manhattan in glorious black and white, set the scene. Willis arrives late at a small gym in downtown New York. He's there to see this incredible fighter (Toro Moreno, played by wrestler Mike Lane) spar a few rounds. Benko starts barking orders. Willis tells him to get to the main event. What he sees leaves a bad taste in his mouth. Other than being an impressive physical specimen, Moreno can't fight. He's slow and ponderous. Doesn't hit very hard. Can't take it either. Willis tells Benko that, "Even against a mediocre heavyweight he'll get beat." Though aggravated, Benko keeps selling, and Willis keeps listening. He's the moral center of the film, a seemingly decent man desperate for work and money—while asking himself how low he'll go to achieve both.

Willis acquiesces. Moreno's fights will be fixed and it will be up to Willis to sell them as the real deal. Moreno rises in the rankings. He starts to believe his own publicity. Until, in one of the best scenes from the film, Willis has George (played by former heavyweight champion Jersey Joe Walcott) knock some reality into Moreno. The big guy is scheduled to fight heavyweight champion Buddy Brannen (strongly played by former champion Max Baer) in a legitimate match. Willis has grown fond of the gentle giant. He doesn't want to see him get hurt by Brannen. Speaking of real, Primo Carnera was handled by mobster Owney Madden for most of his career. There's been debate over the years on how many of Carnera's fights were fixed. Some were not. But there are many ways boxing matches can be fixed. Referees and judges can be bought off. Carnera was left penniless by the mob. *The Harder They Fall* has no gray. Corruption breeds corruption.

The film is ably directed by Mark Robson. The script is tight, with terse dialogue. It has the feel of a documentary at times. Bogart and Steiger are terrific, although their acting styles differ. Reportedly, Bogart, a product of the old, hit your mark and say your lines, thought Steiger, a graduate of the method style of acting, was overacting – so he underplayed his scenes more than usual. The effect is perfect. Bogart's anguish is obvious as his character wrestles with his conscience. Near the end of the film, it's as if he's gargling with razor blades. When he does rage, it's extremely effective. Steiger barks and channels his character's sleaze. The climatic championship fight is savage and cruel. George and Willis had advised Moreno to "go down, and stay down." Moreno doesn't listen. ("What will people think of me?")

The camerawork and editing are especially efficient here, giving the viewer shots of the audience, and tense closeups of the fighters. Lane gives a solid performance as Moreno. You feel for the big lug. He's an innocent caught in the crossfire. *The Harder They Fall* is a hard-hitting look at the corrupt world of boxing. It's interesting to note that around the time the film was made, the mob had its grip securely around the neck of "The Sweet Science." Men like Frankie Carbo worked out of the shadows and set things up.

Another fighter dealing with mob issues and corrupt managers is Mountain Rivera in *Requiem for a Heavyweight*, made in 1962. The story was conceived by New York writer, and former amateur boxer, Rod Serling, a few years before he created "The Twilight Zone." Serling had won an Emmy for his original screenplay *Patterns* in 1955. Serling was hot, so *Requiem*, his follow-up script, was immediately nabbed by producer David Susskind. The resulting television production, staring Jack Palance, received raves for the story and performance by Palance. Seven years later, Columbia Pictures reunited the team of Susskind, director Ralph Nelson, and Serling, for the filmed version. Two-time Academy Award winner Anthony Quinn, picked by Serling, was offered the lead. He quickly accepted. Quinn was a boxing fan. A few years before, he had worked out at the Main Street Gym in Los Angeles and occasionally sparred with Primo Carnera. *Requiem* tells the tale of Rivera, a former contender pushing 40, having to face life after a doctor tells him that one more punch and he'll likely go blind.

The doctor chastises Rivera's manager Maish (Jackie Gleason) for even allowing Rivera to fight. "He had no business in there, Maish," says the doctor. "You hungry or something?" "What do you mean hungry?" Maish says. "In nineteen fifty-two, he was number five." "Nineteen fifty-two?" retorts the doctor. "When was that, Maish? Last Thursday?" Maish ignores him. "Maybe he's lucky at that. At least he walks away with his brains." Rivera accepts the doctor's advice reluctantly. He's been boxing for 25 years. It's all he knows. What's he supposed to do? With the help of his loyal cut man Army (beautifully played by Mickey Rooney) Rivera looks for a job. After a number of rejections, Rivera meets sympathetic employment agent Grace Miller (Julie Harris) who, moved by his story and the obvious kindness of the big ex-fighter, decides to help him find employment.

Meanwhile, Maish is in debt to "Ma" Greeny, a local hood. He knows his days are numbered if he can't pay Ma back. He sabotages

Rivera's job prospects and schemes to get him to wrestle. Army, after discovering Maish's plans, confronts him. "You fink," he says. "You dirty, stinking fink." Later Rivera tells Maish, "I'll do anything for you, but don't ask me to play a clown."

Serling, an admirer of former heavyweight champion Joe Louis, based part of his story on Louis having to wrestle to make money. Quinn is fantastic as the broken, but still breathing, Rivera. Clinging to his pride, Rivera accepts what he is with good humor, determination, and eventually, resignation. His dream is over, but he won't stay down, until he feels he has no choice, due to personal loyalty. Gleason is superb as the sleazy, weak-willed Maish. Though he cares for Rivera, he'll still sell him out. Supposedly Gleason and Quinn clashed over their opposite approach to their roles. Gleason learned his lines on the way to the studio. His photographic memory made such a thing doable. When he was on the set, he was ready to go. He hated rehearsing and was allegedly often boozed up after a night of carousing. Quinn preferred sitting alone, quietly rehearsing his lines. He asked questions, which drove Gleason to distraction. Julie Harris excels in her smart part, emoting a kindness that Rivera is not accustomed to. Director Nelson utilizes the grimness of the characters by keeping things dark and tight. Their futures are bleak and the lack of light intensifies their plight.

For any fan of pugilism, *Requiem for a Heavyweight* can be tough viewing. Writer Budd Schulberg, who also penned the unforgettable *On the Waterfront*, said this about the sport: "As much as I love boxing, I hate it. And as much as I hate it, I love it." Truer words have never been spoken.

These five films dramatically tell the stories of the ups, downs, and dirt of a boxer's career. It's like watching a train wreck, but you can't look away.

What's Next?

By Jerry Fitch

I first started writing about boxing in 1969, sending in local fight reports to *Boxing Illustrated* magazine. From that point on I eventually started submitting feature stories to *Boxing Illustrated*, *The Ring* magazine, and other publications. I had my first full-length feature in 1971, in *Boxing Illustrated*.

Over the years I wrote fight reports and features for many of the more important fight publications including the two mentioned above and others such as *Boxing News* (London, England), *Boxing Digest*, *Boxing World* (South Africa) and *Boxing World* (USA). I also wrote for smaller publications in Toronto, Canada and New Zealand. I was occasionally asked to submit biographical pages for various boxing dinners, even Hall of Fame programs. At one point years ago I kept everything I had ever written in binders, a total of over 600 features, reports and bios. Not bad for a guy who had no formal training as a journalist.

My first book was titled Cleveland's Greatest Fighters of All Time, which I put out in April of 1980. It consisted of just five chapters and thirty pages. I wrote about the fighters I considered the top five in Cleveland boxing history: Johnny Kilbane, Johnny Risko, Lloyd Marshall, Jimmy Bivins and Joey Maxim. Having had 500 copies printed at one of the local quick print places as I was going to a big boxing dinner in Rochester, New York, I thought it would be a great place to sell copies. However I was too busy at the dinner to actually try and sell the book. Eventually I did sell all 500 copies. One of the few I kept I had signed by Lloyd Marshall, Jimmy Bivins and Joey Maxim.

Some twenty years later I did a self-published expanded version of *Cleveland's Greatest Fighters of All Time* called *More Cleveland's Greatest Fighters of All Time*, which I had printed locally at 50 copies a batch. When I needed more I would just order another 50 copies from the printer. Jimmy Bivins' family purchased dozens of copies and took them to family reunions in Georgia, Oklahoma and elsewhere. Jimmy's sister Maria always called it "Jimmy's book," even though Jimmy Bivins was in only one chapter.

Those two books eventually led to my 2002 effort through Arcadia Publishing, also titled *Cleveland's Greatest Fighters of All Time*. I can say in the context of boxing writing the book has been successful. The fact it is still available through Arcadia Publishing, myself and other sites tells me it has done okay.

Since the Arcadia effort in 2002 I have written four other books and this current one makes a total of six, eight if you consider my first two "Cleveland's Greatest" efforts. While I do not consider myself a prolific writer I must say that even when I was writing for several magazines at the same time in the 1970s, I could never have envisioned that someday I would ever have written this many books. After all I can safely say boxing writing, in most cases, has always been a hobby. There is no other way to describe it.

When it came time to consider writing another book I found myself stuck for any good ideas. Since my last book *My Favorite Fighters* came out in December of 2018, I really felt like I just needed a break. Although there are a few fighters I might have considered for a biographical type effort, as I had done with Jimmy Bivins and Johnny Risko, I just couldn't seem to get excited about any particular subject. I felt I had come to a dead end.

Most of my writing comes from ideas that often just pop into my head. Unlike being a newspaper guy, freelancing as I have always done requires nobody telling me what to write or when. Although people have suggested ideas to me, none of my books have ever been forced upon me by anyone but myself. My influences come from more than 60 years of following boxing. In my case I started following boxing in the mid to late 1950s.

Although encouraged at times by a few of my supporters of my work who have said, "What's Next?," I really was not in the mood. I didn't want to try and force something that just was not there.

From time-to-time I even thought maybe my writing days for the most part were over. I retired from a regular job in October of 2008. But how do you retire from something that really isn't work in the truest sense?

I have of course had more time to write in actual retirement. But I also have had time to do a lot of wonderful things like travel and spend quality time in my city enjoying local culture, sports and other events. Often Lynda and I say "How could we possibly have had time to do all of the things we do now, when we worked?" The answer is simple, we did not have the time to do it during our working lives.

Still just because I have more free time, especially since as I write this we are going through a global pandemic, that does not mean I have all of the answers or ideas about what to write. Writing just for the sake of writing makes no sense to me.

Then one day out of the blue I casually mentioned to fellow writer and friend, John Raspanti that I wouldn't mind co-authoring a book. I never considered such a thing seriously before so it came as a shock to me that those words came out of my mouth. I then thought why not? I have seen many successful books that were co-authored. My son Tad has been involved in many such efforts with his Titanic books and other maritime stories.

I knew that John Raspanti had been successful as a co-author with Dennis Taylor in their well received book *Intimate Warfare: The True Story of the Arturo Gatti and Mikey Ward Boxing Trilogy*. I also knew John loved boxing and I had good experiences with John as we reviewed each other's books over the last several years.

At first I don't think John believed I was serious about being a co-author. But when I convinced him I was, we didn't take long to jump right into the fray. So we decided to take a leap of faith and work together on a new book.

It seems when I am finished with a book, especially the last couple, I truly start thinking that it could possibly be the last one. I have a strong feeling I will feel the same way after this book. This is not to say it hasn't been rewarding working with John. Quite the opposite, it has been fun. John and I have an age gap and different writing styles and for the most part he has watched and covered boxing far more recently than I have. He has a whole new slant on things. It is refreshing. Working with him has been a blast.

If you will forgive me I will simply say I have no intentions of writing another book at this time. When asked "What's Next?" I will simply say I never say never...

Memories Of The Olympic Auditorium

By John J. Raspanti

The first time I visited Southern California's boxing's mecca was when I was 14. I returned for another look 42 years later.

The Olympic Auditorium opened for business in 1925. Heavyweight champion Jack Dempsey, and matinee idol Rudolph Valentino, were in attendance. Dempsey had initiated the groundbreaking ceremony the year before. The venue sits at the corner of 18th and Grand in the shadow of the Santa Monica freeway.

Hollywood immediately recognized the "look" of the Olympic. Silent movie comedian Buster Keaton ventured out of his studio in 1926 to film the boxing comedy *Battling Butler* there. Seventy-eight years later, Clint Eastwood shot scenes for *Million Dollar Baby* at the Olympic.

In the early seventies, every Saturday night, just after midnight, I'd fiddle with the rabbit ears of my tiny black and white television attempting to tune in the fights from the Olympic. I was usually successful, though I'd sometimes miss a bout or two. The audio would come in first. It would be such a relief to hear ringside commentator, Jim Healy. I could usually tell how important a fight was based on how Healy was expressing himself.

The grainy look of my old colorless television was a perfect way to watch the fights. In a way it was like going back in time. The ring, the holder of many bloody battles, was old and faded. I was always fascinated by a banner that hung over the ring - displaying a phone number (RI-9-5171). I had dreamed of one day seeing it in person.

The dream came true a few days before a trip to Reno with my family. We arrived on a Thursday at my grandparents' home in Rosemead, CA. The fights would go down the next night. I mentioned the Olympic and fights to my dad. He nodded, but as was his way, didn't commit. I'll admit to nagging him a little. The following day, he told grampa and me that he had bought tickets for the fights. I can remember losing my breath when he told us. I was finally going to see the place in person.

LA is one big freeway so it didn't take us long to get there. Excepting the traffic, of course. Rosemead is roughly twenty miles from the Olympic. I was really curious to see the outside of the arena. I had recently seen a picture of the place from the 1940s. I spotted the faded white building a few blocks away. It was huge, encapsulating the entire corner of 18th and Grand. I remember the marquee was gold with red letters. Oscar "Shotgun" Alvarado and Andy "The Hawk" Price were the headliners.

"The first time I saw the Olympic I was maybe twelve or thirteen. My dad, my brother, and I watched the fights every Thursday, and I thought it was a great place 'cause it was so rowdy."

- *Former welterweight champion of the world Carlos Palomino.*

Rowdy is right. As we made our way inside and through the lobby, people around us shoved and grumbled. Perhaps it was because I had slowed down and was gawking at the pictures on the walls. Many were legends. Seconds later, a roar erupted. The fights had started.

"A historic place. The walls outside with the pictures of Jack Dempsey and others...and inside the arena all along the walkways that circumvent the building...pictures of the greatest fighters of the century...and of course the ring right in the center of the walkway."

- *Uncrowned welterweight champion Armando Muniz.*

As we made our way to our seats, I couldn't take my eyes off the ring. It looked bigger than it did in pictures. I could see dried blood in both corners. The banner with the phone number was clouded by smoke hovering over the ring like a giant halo. I felt the electricity. Grampa took in the place quietly as we located our seats

15 feet from the ring. A few weeks before our trip, I read about the historic battle between former champions Mando Ramos (one of my favorites) and Sugar Ramos at the Olympic. Blood splatter was everywhere that night. Mando Ramos had cuts over both eyes and a bloody nose. Sugar Ramos's face was lumpy and damaged. Mando dug down deep and won the final round and the fight. The sellout crowd screamed itself hoarse.

The fighters got ready for the bout below the arena. One fight was in the books. The impatient crowd stomped their collective feet. Suddenly the fighters appeared.

"First time I fought there was as an amateur. This was in the days that the amateurs and pros fought on the same card. I took everything in. The building was huge and old. To get to the dressing room you had to walk down the main corridor and go down four to six steps to a plateau. A chalkboard was there with the fighter's names and dressing rooms on it. It was very dense in there. The entire building was made of cement. The walls near the dressing rooms had blood on them. You knew what was going on above by the sounds. They were all different. A huge roar meant a knockout. Whistles were for a hot chick. The building would rumble as you tried to sleep. Almost every one of my fights ended in a riot."

- Former amateur star and NABF welterweight champion, Randy Shields.

The crowd booed as undefeated prospect Andy "The Hawk" Price stepped into the squared circle. I can remember being surprised by the reaction of the crowd. The guy could fight. He often appeared at the Olympic and was managed by Burt Reynolds, Lee Majors, and Marvin Gaye. I spotted Gaye near Price's corner. So did the crowd. Some cheered him. Price was super quick and flashy. He was more boxer than puncher. He pranced around the ring in his red velvet robe full of confidence.

"When I was growing up, my brothers and I would go on Wednesday to watch wrestling. Thursday was boxing. Our favorite seats were way in the back near the hot dog stand where all the gamblers would sit. They made it very exciting talking trash and screaming foul language at the fighters for not living up to their expectations."

- Former lightweight champion Genaro Hernandez.

Price fought unknown Lou Blades who drew cheers as he waved to the crowd. Fans love underdogs and Blades did come to fight. He chased Price for six rounds, but never came close to caching him. Price won by wide decision. The crowd booed some more. He didn't seem to notice. Price would go on to defeat future champions Carlos Palomino and Pipino Cuevas. Though blessed with solid boxing skills, his lack of power and suspect chin doomed him. His last chance at glory was against Sugar Ray Leonard in 1979. Leonard took him out in the first round.

"When I was at the Olympic in the 1960s it was wild ass crowd. Lots of drunk people. They would fill up their cups up with piss and throw em. There were fights in the crowd and parking lot. There was a little hot dog stand next to the Olympic. All the trainers met there. I'd just sit and listen to them talk. They were like absolute Gods to me."

- Former Diamond Belt Amateur Champion and timekeeper John Liechy.

The main event started mere minutes after the Price fight. Dad bought a program and popcorn. He read to us what it said about Oscar "Shotgun" Albarado, but I already knew quite a bit about Albarado. Two years before, I watched his fight on TV against my favorite, Armando Muniz, at the Olympic. Muniz was undefeated at the time. Albarado had won 35 of 39 fights. He'd thrown hands with contenders Adolph Pruitt, and Hedgemon Lewis. The guy could punch. His left hook was deadly. Albarado was a throwback fighter, willing to take three to land one. He landed plenty that night, but so did Muniz. The fight was a 10-round war. Each fighter rocked each other multiple times. The judges scored the match a draw. I thought about that as Albarado made his way to the ring. The roar was huge. Albarado was fighting a guy named Dino Del Cid, who three weeks before at this same venue, had upset Albarado. Del Cid was in the ring as well and looking plenty nervous.

"It took me an hour and half to get there. I had butterflies before I fought. It was amazing for me to think of all the famous fighters that had fought there. Then I'd go to the catacombs below the seats. I called it the dungeon. Concrete walls. It was cold down there. Gave you cold feeling. I had to warm up. I'd try to listen to music to get the butterflies away. I'd hear a rumbling and wonder who got knocked out. You never saw anything. You just heard it. I'd see some celebrities and they'd wave to me. That would psych me up. I wish I could go back in time. I loved that place."

- Former welterweight contender Herman Montes.

The aggressive Albarado, black hair, black eyes, and black trunks, wasted little time taking it to Del Cid. He fired left hooks at random. Many missed, but just as many landed with a thud. Del Cid was hurt. The crowd screamed. Dad, Grampa, and me stood and watched Albarado hunt Del Cid. Another whistling left floored Del Cid. He bravely got up, but seconds later was down again. The sound was so loud it felt like the roof was going to fly off. Del Cid was down again right before the round ended. Somehow, he pulled himself up. His corner worked him over the best they could. He stood like a zombie; his eyes glassy like a guy who had had one to many. He had. Albarado tore into him and ended things. Impressive and deadly. A year later he'd win the junior middleweight world title. I was happy for Albarado. The guy was a real warrior.

As we made our way out, I kept glancing back at the ring. A guy with a broom was sweeping up some leftover coins, thrown in the ring by the fans. I saw him put a few in his pocket.

I can hear the fans cheer and boo as I walked down towards the ring. This made me excited and frightened at the same time, but my adrenaline was pumping so hard that I knew I was ready to fight in that ring and knew I was going to do well.

  - Former lightweight contender Tony Baltazar.

Some forty years later, I gaze at what remains of the Olympic. It rises skyward from its corner lot like a looming presence from another time. Now, it's a house of worship even though its ticket booths still stand under layers of dirt and grime.

"I loved it there. Walking through those tunnels out of the dressing rooms. It was awesome-knowing you were walking in history with past fighters. Then the crowd cheers. It was like night and day. I sure miss the Olympic. It was sad to see it go."

  - Former super lightweight champion Zachary Padilla.

I sneak inside and spot where our seats were so long ago. I strain to hear the roar of the crowd. A podium sits where names like Quarry, Moore, Liston, Frazier, Norton, Griffith, Patterson, Canzoneri, Chacon, Lopez, Ramos, Palomino, Cuevas, and Muniz all battled.

The irony doesn't escape me. The Olympic will always be a cathedral of blood, guts, determination, and most of all, memories.

Photo Credits

Front cover photo by John J. Raspanti

Page 11   Tony Zale and Jerry Fitch (Author's Collection)

Page 23   Anton Christoforidis (Jerry Fitch Author's Collection)

Page 30   Jimmy Bivins (Jerry Fitch Author's Collection)

Page 33   Street Sign (Photo by Jerry Fitch)

Page 51   Jimmy McLarnin (Jerry Fitch Author's Collection)

Page 53   Floyd Patterson (Jerry Fitch Author's Collection)

Page 55   Joey Giardello (Jerry Fitch Author's Collection)

Page 58   Joe Frazier and Jerry Fitch (Photo by Tony Liccione)

Page 60   Emile Griffith (Jerry Fitch Author's Collection)

Page 65   Larry Holmes (Jerry Fitch Author's Collection)

Page 66   Jimmy Bivins and Jerry Fitch (Author's Collection)

Page 72   Doyle Baird (Jerry Fitch Author's Collection)

Page 74   Ernie Terrell (Jerry Fitch Author's Collection)

Page 78   Frankie Wallace (Jerry Fitch Author's Collection)

Page 88   Jersey Joe Walcott and Jerry Fitch (Author's Collection)

Page 90   George Pace (Photo Credit Charlie Harris-Plain Dealer, 1978)

Page 93   Joey Maxim-Archie Moore (Jerry Fitch Author's Collection)

Page 97   Jerry Fitch and Lloyd Marshall (Photo by Terry Gallagher)

Page 100   Frankie Garcia (Jerry Fitch Author's Collection)

Page 107   Rory Calhoun-Randy Sandy (Jerry Fitch Author's Collection)

Page 110   Willie Troy (Jerry Fitch Author's Collection)

Page 122   Jake LaMotta-Laurent Dauthuille (Courtesy of *Plain Dealer* from Cleveland News Reference Department, 9-18-50)

Page 123   Fight Ticket (Jerry Fitch Author's Collection)

Page 128   Jerry Fitch and Alexis Arguello (Photo by Tony Liccione)

Page 25   Ring Of Fire (John J. Raspanti (Author's Collection)

Page 38   Karim Mayfield and John J. Raspanti (Author's Collection)

Page 49   Virgil Hunter and John J. Raspanti (Author's Collection)

Page 70   Robert Guerrero and John J. Raspanti (Author's Collection)

Page 71   Israel Vasquez and John J. Raspanti (Author's Collection)

ALSO BY JERRY FITCH

Cleveland's Greatest Fighters of All Time

James Louis Bivins...The Man Who Would Be Champion

50 Years of Fights, Fighters and Friendships

Johnny Risko...The Cleveland Rubber Man

My Favorite Fights

ALSO BY JOHN J. RASPANTI

Intimate Warfare: The True Story of the Arturo Gatti and Micky Ward Boxing Trilogy (co-author Dennis Taylor)

Blood On My Notebook: Dispatches From the World of Professional Boxing

www.ingramcontent.com/pod-product-compliance
Lightning Source LLC
Chambersburg PA
CBHW021336090426
42742CB00008B/626